A Sailor's Guide to Sails

A Sailor's Guide to Sails

SVEN DONALDSON

DODD, MEAD & COMPANY NEW YORK

Published by Dodd, Mead & Company, Inc.
79 Madison Avenue, New York, N.Y. 10016
Distributed in Canada by
McClelland and Stewart Limited, Toronto
Manufactured in the United States of America
Designed by Nancy Dale Muldoon
First Edition

Library of Congress Cataloging in Publication Data

Donaldson, Sven.
A sailor's guide to sails.
Includes index.
1. Sails. I. Title.
VM532.D65 1984 623.8'62 83-14063
ISBN 0-396-08190-8
ISBN 0-396-08199-1 (pbk.)

To my father, DAVID DONALDSON,
who introduced me to sailboats and sailboat racing

CONTENTS

A Sailor's Guide to Sails

Introduction

A Sailor's Guide to Sails originated in early 1982 with a suggestion from Paul Burkhart, editor of *Pacific Yachting* magazine, that I consider writing a series of articles on "state of the art" sailmaking. As the idea evolved, we decided it was important that the series present the fundamentals of sail technology, as well as the newest developments.

The twelve articles that appeared in *Pacific Yachting*, together with several articles on sail trim I had written earlier for the same publication, were the basis of this book. First and foremost, it is an attempt to communicate, in the simplest possible language, what to a sailmaker is common knowledge. As is the case with most professions, the specialized jargon of the sailmaking trade is a formidable smoke screen that could easily unnerve a newcomer. For this reason, I have identified and defined important terms as they appear in the text, as well as providing a comprehensive glossary.

The ideas and information presented in the twelve chapters that follow are extensively interrelated. For this reason, I recommend that the reader proceed through the book from the beginning, rather than examine a chapter here and a chapter there as specific needs or questions arise. To make the task as easy as possible, I've tried to avoid dwelling on individual topics, even my favorites. *A Sailor's Guide to Sails* is meant to be an introduction, not a reference book.

I am well aware that not every sailor will wish to have his or her romantic concepts of sailing "spoiled" by even the most lighthearted sort of technological analysis. On the other hand, for those who are intrigued by how things work, I hope you will find something here to enjoy. Happy sailing.

I wish to thank the staff at *Pacific Yachting* for their encouragement and editorial suggestions. To Gerry Storch, Dave Miller, George Wilkens, and the other sailmakers I have worked with and learned from, my thanks as well. Much credit is also due Sandra Millen for the valuable assistance she provided in refining the text and preparing illustrations. Lastly, I owe a real debt to all the skilled sailors who have furthered my education by sailing with and against me.

1 Fundamentals

THE objective of this book is to provide recreational sailors with enough up-to-date technical knowledge to be able to purchase and use sails intelligently. It is written as an introduction, not an encyclopedic reference for the expert, nor as a primer for the would-be amateur sailmaker.

Casual sail users frequently have little or no idea of how sails work. Many believe that the design and manufacture of sails is a black art. In contrast, enthusiasts of cameras and hi-fi equipment usually understand their equipment quite thoroughly, despite its obviously greater complexity. Of course the benefits of understanding everyday technology are substantial. Knowing something about cars, cameras, and household appliances, for example, makes it possible to purchase wisely, minimize maintenance costs, and generally derive more utility and enjoyment from ownership. This also applies to sails.

Knowledgeable customers are an asset to sailmakers as well as to themselves. Since sails are, for the most part, produced or distributed by small businesses that deal with clients on a first-hand basis, it is a blessing to have customers who "speak the language" and understand the unique nature of the sailmaking trade.

This first chapter presents important fundamentals and

provides an overview of the types of sails ordinarily encountered on modern sailboats. Of course, a far wider array of sail types has been used over the long history of sailing. Traditional sailing craft are still in use today all over the world, but any attempt to deal with such diversity (not to mention the accompanying vocabularies) would far exceed the scope of this book. In fact, neither the basic principles of sailing, nor those of sail design have changed much over the centuries. Most of the information offered has fairly universal applicability in the sailing world.

ANATOMY OF A SAIL

Most modern sails are triangular sheets of flexible material held in a more or less vertical plane by spars or combinations of spars and rigging wires. The forward or more upwind edge of a sail is called its LUFF; the more downwind edge, the LEECH, and the lower edge, the FOOT (Figure 1.1). In practice, the leech almost invariably forms the actual trailing edge of the sailing airfoil, but the luff only occasionally corresponds to the real aerodynamic leading edge, because a spar, wire, or luff rod of some kind typically lies ahead of it. To further complicate matters, the terms luff, leech, and foot are also used to refer to broad regions of the sail in the vicinity of the respective edges; and the word luff when employed as a verb, has additional meanings altogether. The corner of a sail where the luff intersects the foot is called the TACK. The luff/leech intersection and the leech/foot intersection are called the HEAD and CLEW respectively. When any normal sail is spread out on a level surface, it will immediately be obvious that none of the three edges is a straight line. The curvature of the luff is particularly important in determining the three-dimensional shape that a sail will assume when set normally in a

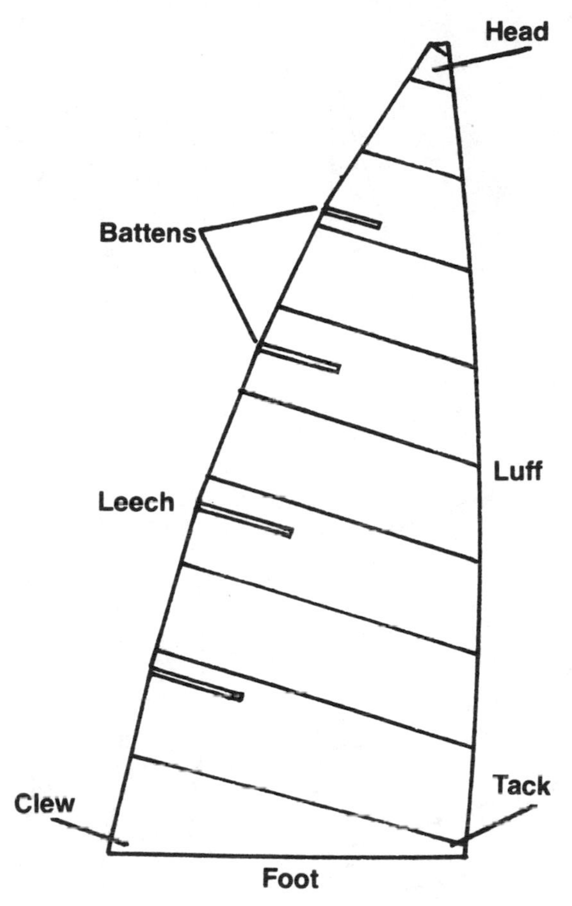

Figure 1.1 Parts of a sail.

boat's rig. Laid out on the floor, the luff curve can appear either convex, concave, or S-shaped (a combination of both). Leech curves can be either convex or concave. Since convex leeches are inherently unstable as compared to concave ones, stiffening rods called BATTENS must often be used to support this extra sail area (ordinarily called ROACH). Foot curves too can be either convex or concave, with a slight convexity being the norm.

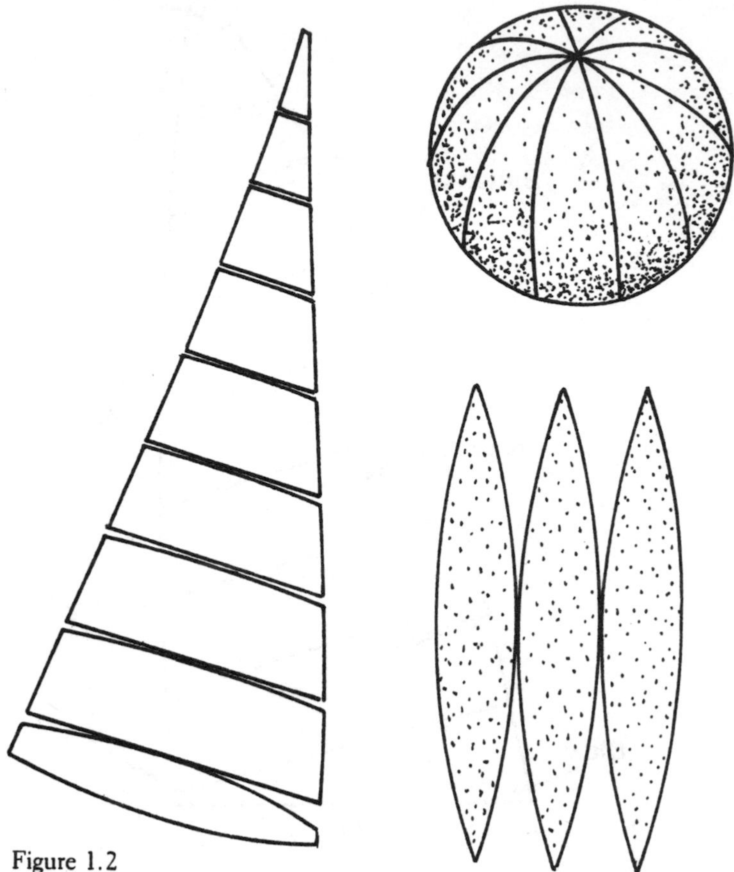

Figure 1.2
The three-dimensional curvature of most sails is generated like that of a beach ball. In each case, tapered panels cut from flat stock are joined along the edges.

A normal sail, spread out on a level surface cannot be induced to lie flat, for the same reason that a deflated beach ball will not lie flat. Both the sail and the beach ball are built from doubly tapered strips of flat material attached together at their edges—a construction technique that generates a close approximation of smooth compound or multidirectional curvature (Figure 1.2). In the case of the beach ball, individual panels are tapered so extensively that the ends of each lens-shaped sector come to a point. The panels of sails are much more subtly tapered, and the amount of compound curvature generated is consequently much reduced.

Set on a boat's rig, every sail assumes a three-dimensional curved shape. This curvature is called CAMBER (alternatively DRAFT or FLOW), and can be evaluated by looking at cross sections of the sail at various levels. A straight line from luff to leech at some particular height is called a CHORD (Figure 1.3). The greatest perpendicular distance from a chord to the surface of the sail itself is called the DEPTH. The DEPTH-TO-CHORD RATIOS or CAMBER RATIOS at different heights in a sail are crucial determinants of its aerodynamic characteristics (Figure 1.4). Also important are the MAXIMUM DEPTH LOCATIONS; the fore-and-aft positions of the deepest points in the camber at the various heights in the sail.

In essence, a sail can be envisioned as a stack of curved shapes, each described by its camber ratio and maximum depth location. Conventional practice, however, is to de-

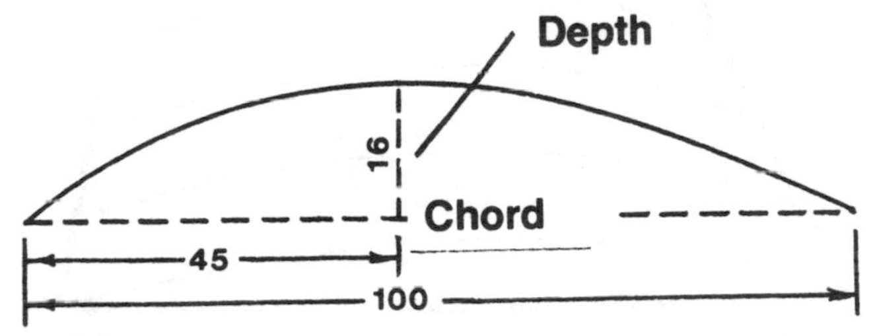

Figure 1.3
Depth/chord ratio and maximum depth location are important features of sail camber. In this example, depth/chord ratio is 0.16 or 16 percent. Maximum depth location is 45 percent aft, or 45 percent of the chord length behind the luff.

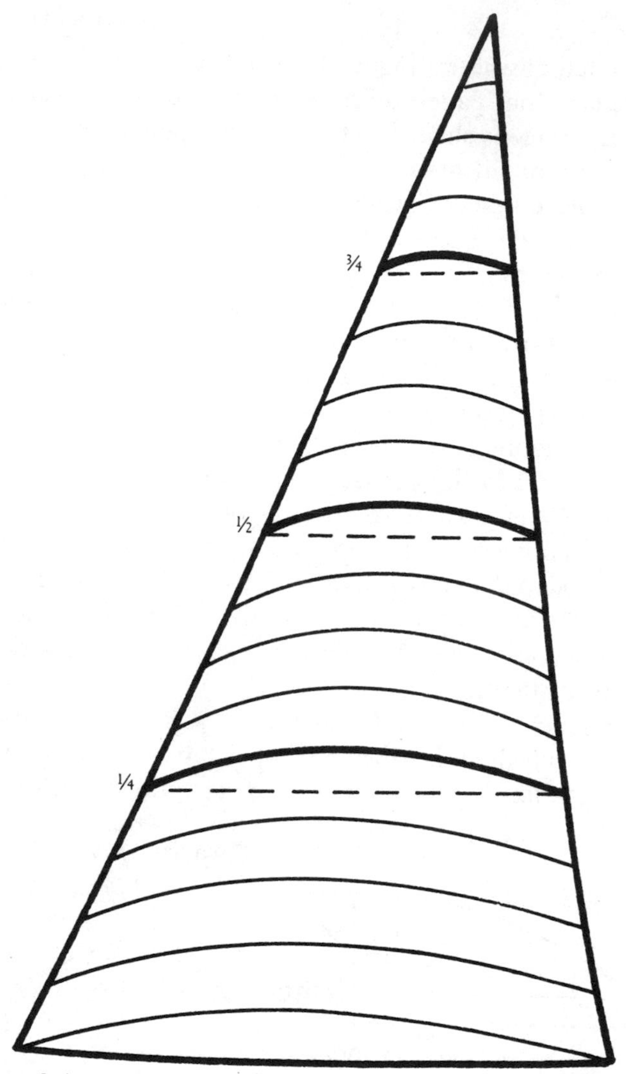

Figure 1.4
The three-dimensional shape of a sail is best envisioned as a stack of cambered shapes, each with its own depth/chord ratio and maximum depth location. However, in most cases, the overall shape of a sail can be adequately evaluated by determining the camber at the quarter heights.

scribe a sail by measuring these data at only three heights: one fourth, one half, and three fourths of the distance up the luff. Both camber ratios and maximum depth locations are ordinarily expressed as percentages of chord length. Thus the phrase "16 percent camber, 45 percent aft" means that at a particular chord or height, the sail in question has a depth/chord ratio of 0.16 and that the deepest point in its camber is located 45 percent of the chord length aft of the luff. As it turns out, the acceptable range of camber ratios and maximum draft locations for good sailing performance is surprisingly restrictive. Sails with depth/chord ratios that tend toward the higher end of the spectrum are called FULL sails, while those with low depth/chord ratios are described as FLAT.

A SAIL BY ANY OTHER NAME

Modern sailboats, almost without exception, are rigged as catboats, sloops, cutters, ketches, or yawls (Figure 1.5). All of these carry a MAINSAIL which today is usually of the Marconi type—basically triangular in shape and attached along the entire length of the luff to the aft edge of a more or less vertical spar. Although the mainsail is often not the largest sail carried by a modern yacht, it is important because it is used in all sailing conditions except, perhaps, extreme storm. It is therefore desirable to be able to alter the camber of a mainsail from relatively full to quite flat. Achieving this end is quite tricky in practice, and it is common to relinquish some control in exchange for simplicity and economy. The only real exception to the single mainsail principle is the laudable practice of carrying a very small, strongly constructed storm mainsail called a TRYSAIL.

CAT RIGS, rigs which concentrate 100 percent of their

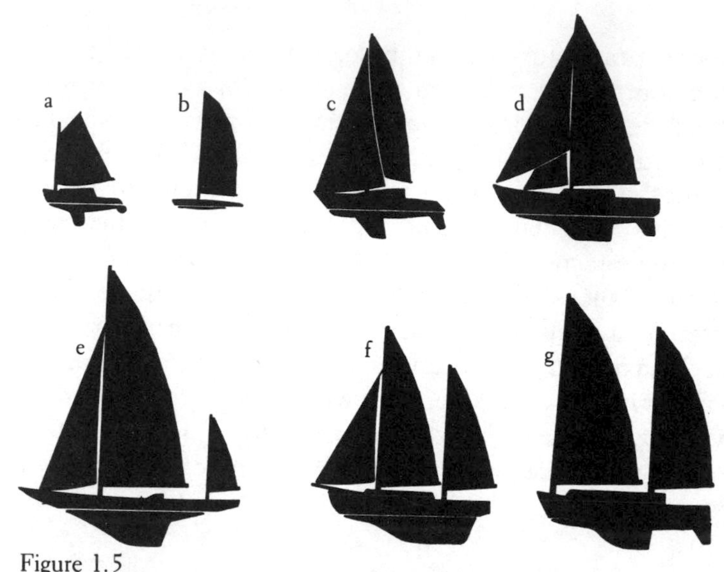

Figure 1.5
Modern sailing rigs in common use includes: cat rigs (a), una rigs (b), sloops (c), cutters (d), yawls (e), ketches (f), and cat ketches (g).

sail area into a single mainsail, are currently enjoying a resurgence of popularity. The propulsive efficiency of a cat sail largely depends upon the size and shape of the spar that forms its leading edge. If the leading edge profile is sufficiently refined, as in the case of the sophisticated, rotating wing spars used on very high-performance catamarans, a refined cat rig or UNA RIG can generate more forward thrust per unit of sail area than any other type. Drawbacks of these rigs generally include difficulty in achieving adequate control of sail shape and area, and excessive weight aloft.

The so-called CAT KETCH RIG is basically two cat sails on separate spars arranged one behind the other. Unless these spars are unusually sophisticated and small in section, cat ketch rigs are quite inefficient for the area of sail they carry. However, they are extremely easy to handle.

All other rig types in common use incorporate one or

more HEADSAILS—sails supported along their luffs by sloping wire HEADSTAYS. In comparison to most mainsails, headsails boast leading edges that are aerodynamically clean. Consequently they usually can generate more forward thrust per unit of area than mainsails can. The majority of present-day sailboats are SLOOPS—boats that ordinarily use only one headsail at a time. Few sloops larger than dinghys use a single headsail in all conditions. Most carry a variety of headsails: larger, fuller ones for lower wind speeds; smaller, flatter ones for stronger blows; and in some cases, specialized sails for reaching vs. closehauled sailing at various wind velocities.

Headsails that overlap the mast are called GENOAS (sometimes capitalized in recognition of the Italian city where sails of this type were perhaps first used). It is conventional to describe the size of a genoa by expressing the distance from the clew to the closest point on the luff (length perpendicular or LP MEASUREMENT) as a percentage of the horizontal distance from the headstay intersection with deck back to the front face of the mast (J MEASUREMENT). Thus a genoa with an LP measurement of 6 meters set on a boat with a J measurement of 4 meters is a 150% percent genoa (Figure 1.6).

The largest overlapping headsail in the inventory of a large contemporary sloop is called the #1 GENOA because it is the first in a series of downward steps in headsail area that are taken in sequence as wind speed increases. However, confusion can arise, because it has become common practice for racing yachts to carry two or even three #1 genoas, all of the same area, but subtly different in camber, maximum depth location, and cloth weight.

A smaller overlapping headsail, used when the wind is a little too strong for a boat to sail efficiently with a #1 genoa, is called a #2 GENOA, or in the Caribbean chartering trade,

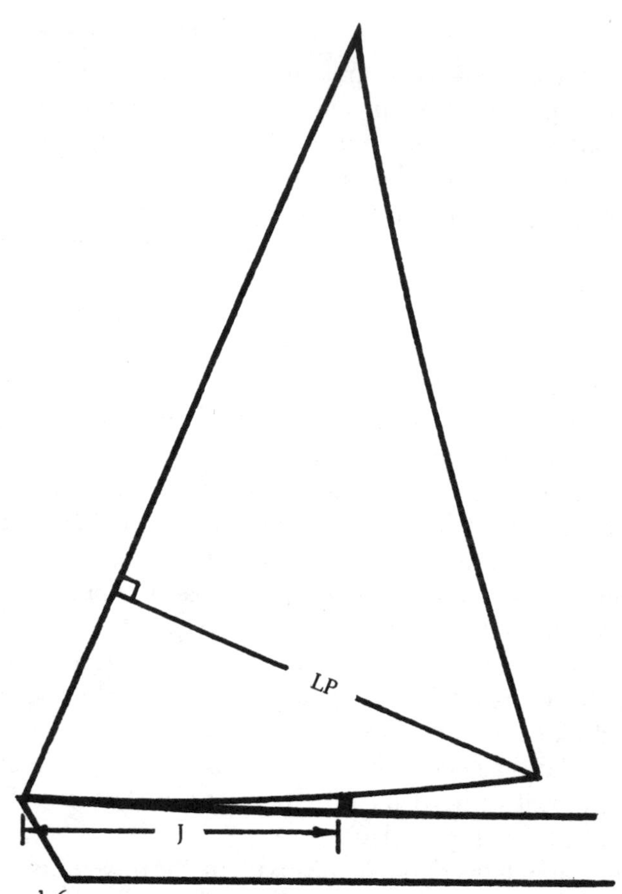

Figure 1.6
LP or "length perpendicular" is the minimum distance from clew to luff. Headsail girth is usually expressed as the ratio of LP to J (the horizontal distance from the base of the headstay to the front face of the mast).

a WORKING GENOA. Modern #2 genoas are virtually as long on the luff as #1 genoas, but have smaller LP measurements. The alternative configuration—a short hoist, large LP sail called a MULE—has gone out of fashion, because experience has shown that luff length is the most important determinant of how much drive a sail generates.

Smaller #2 genoas, usually between 110 percent and 120 percent LP/J are sometimes called LAPPERS.

Non-overlapping headsails are called JIBS. Again, however, terminology has become uncertain as a result of the recent practice of referring to non-overlapping, racing headsails as #3 and #4 genoas; perhaps with the intention of distinguishing them from cruising sails of about the same size. The #3 headsail on a modern ocean racer or racer/cruiser is also sometimes called a BLADE because of its tall, narrow shape.

Extremely heavy weather calls for a very small, strong headsail called, sensibly enough, a STORM JIB.

The single-masted sailboats called CUTTERS use two headsails simultaneously for upwind sailing: a jib on the outer forestay and a STAYSAIL on the inner one. Today, the "true" cutter rig is generally associated with cruising rather than with racing or racing/cruising boats, but the distinction between sloops and cutters is again a fuzzy one. Many cruising cutters today use a #1 genoa set alone on the outer headstay in light to moderate winds, and only change to a double-headed rig when the wind pipes up. On the other side of the coin, offshore racing sloops routinely set staysails for offwind sailing. Although these racing staysails are free luff sails (since sloops lack an inner forestay), they are essentially the same as the staysails of "true" cutters.

Racing staysails come in a great variety of sizes and shapes and sport an even larger assortment of names: tallboy, banana, dual, and dazy being a few of the most common. To detail their features and specific applications is beyond the scope of this book. Staysails for upwind sailing and close reaching have considerably less camber than the headsails set in front of them because the sail ahead "bends the wind" and creates a local header in the area where the staysail must operate (Figure 1.7). For the same reason, the

Figure 1.7
Forward sails bend the wind for sails behind which accordingly must be built with less camber and trimmed closer to the midline of the boat.

mainsails of sloops and cutters are flatter than the headsails of these boats, particularly when the sails overlap extensively.

In general, when several sails are set simultaneously, the efficiency of those in front increases somewhat, but those behind suffer considerably. However, the value of a particular rig configuration involves more than just the magnitude of the propulsive forces it generates. The use of a double-headed rig, for example, keeps the areas of individual sails within reasonable limits and greatly simplifies sail handling. The crew of a cutter can easily reduce sail simply by dropping one headsail to deck and bagging it where it lies.

The total sail area of YAWLS and KETCHES—the so-called DIVIDED RIGS—is fragmented still further. The MIZZENS of these boats are essentially small mainsails. Being located aft of all other sails in the rig, mizzens must be the flattest of all if they are to be of any conceivable value for upwind work. Staysails and spinnakers can, of course, be flown from the mizzen mast for offwind sailing. Mizzens are often constructed quite heavily, so they can be used in conjunction with just a storm jib for heavy weather.

Nowadays, SPINNAKERS are used extensively for beam reaching, broad reaching, and running in all but the strongest winds. Spinnakers are free luff sails in the truest sense; the spinnaker luff is supported by neither a wire nor a spar, and constitutes the actual leading edge of an airfoil. Ordinarily a spinnaker is tethered to the boat only at its head, tack, and clew. As a result, the sail can bulge laterally outward, permitting greater sail area to be accommodated within the confines of a given rig.

There are basically two types of spinnakers. Conventional or racing type sails are symmetrical to the left and right of a vertical center line. Cruising spinnakers are not (see Figure 1.8).

The tack of a racing type spinnaker is normally held in position by a strong pole projecting perpendicularly from the mast. Racing type spinnakers are fuller or flatter, lighter or heavier for various wind angles and velocities. A modern offshore racing boat carries a number of spinnakers for different conditions, just as it carries a selection of headsails. Racing type spinnakers can, of course, be used for cruising and day sailing as well.

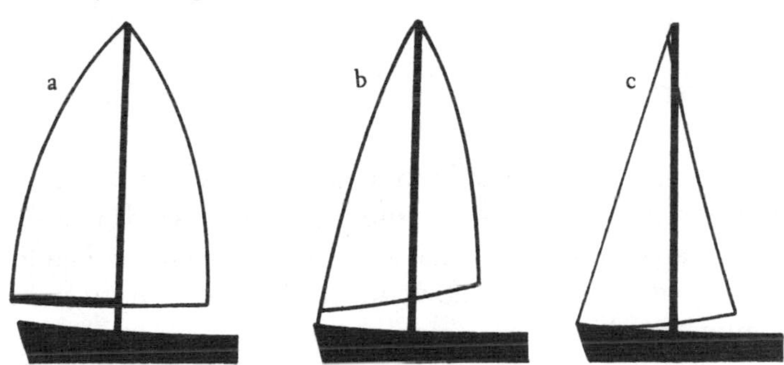

Figure 1.8
Conventional or racing type spinnakers (a) are symmetrical from one side to the other. An asymmetrical cruising spinnaker (b) can be regarded as a cross between a conventional spinnaker and a genoa (c).

The BLOOPER is a free luff sail flown in conjunction with a spinnaker, but on the leeward side of the boat's headstay. According to current race regulations, bloopers are measured as genoas. However, they are designed and built to be as much like spinnakers as possible. Like racing staysails, they are specialty sails, and cannot be justified in most sail lockers.

Cruising spinnakers are, in general, smaller sails than their racing equivalents with leeches that are shorter than their luffs. Unlike racing type spinnakers, the tack of a cruising spinnaker is not held away from the boat with a pole, but is simply tethered to the bow with a line. It is realistic to think of a cruising spinnaker as a hybrid that lies somewhere between a headsail and a spinnaker. Like biological crossbreeds, a cruising spinnaker will usually resemble one "parent" more than the other. It is quite feasible to build cruising spinnakers that are quite genoa-like, perhaps even attached to the headstay here and there. Alternatively, it is equally practical to design very spinnaker-like ones. In any case, performance in some sailing conditions will most certainly be compromised. Sail design is inevitably a game of juggling trade-offs.

A HOLISTIC SAIL INVENTORY

Sailboats need to be able to perform safely and presentably in a variety of sailing conditions. Gentle winds require sails or sail combinations that are physically light enough to fill in the first place, and powerful enough to get the boat up to an acceptable speed. Strong winds demand strong sails that produce large enough forward forces to generate respectable speed, yet maintain heeling forces within acceptable limits; since most sailboats either slow down drastically if heeled excessively, or worse yet, capsize and stop.

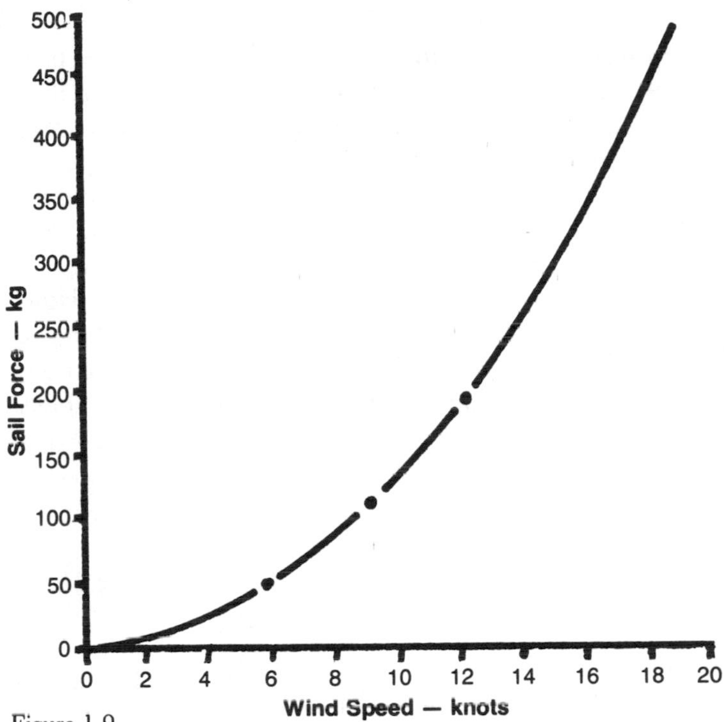

Figure 1.9
Sail forces increase exponentially with increasing wind speed.

To achieve acceptable all-weather performance is actually far more difficult than it might at first appear. For one thing, the forces generated by a sail of a given size, fixed camber, and unvarying trim, increase radically with even a small increase in wind speed (Figure 1.9). A genoa that generates a "lifting force" of 50 kg. in six knots of breeze would theoretically generate 113 kg. when the wind builds to nine knots, and 200 kg. at twelve knots! In practice, the increase is usually still greater, because the camber of a typical genoa increases as the sail is subjected to greater wind loads.

To keep the forces generated by sailboat rigs within tolerable limits, it is crucial to be able to substantially alter both sail area and sail shape to accommodate different sailing conditions. Area changes are, of course, achieved by reefing, dousing, or changing to smaller sails. Sail shape changes are achieved using a variety of control techniques: mast bend, headstay sag, sheet lead angles, differential tension deliberately induced in the fabric of sails, and several others. These will be discussed in Chapters 3 and 9. However, before investigating the finer points of sail camber and camber control, it is helpful to understand how air flows past sails and combinations of sails, generating usable forces in the process.

2 How Sails Work

IT isn't necessary to understand the principles of sail function in order to sail—even to sail well. A sail that is correctly trimmed according to rote rules is just as effective as one that is correctly and "scientifically" trimmed. Nevertheless, it can be helpful as well as satisfying to really know what's going on in the rig overhead.

If you find the very thought of physics terrifying, the value of this book will not be seriously compromised if you skip ahead to Chapter 3. On the other hand, I urge you to have a go at it first. Physics is the most down-to-earth of the sciences—basic rules that govern the behavior of literally everything. The principles of sailing are solidly rooted in everyday experience and, for the most part, can be grasped intuitively.

FORCES AND FLUIDS

Sailboats are machines that extract energy from the movement of the wind with respect to the water, and convert some of that energy into the energy of boat motion. Sails are nothing more than sophisticated flow obstructions, carefully designed to alter the direction and speed of the passing air to produce a net LIFTING FORCE acting in a diagonally forward direction (see Figure 2.1).

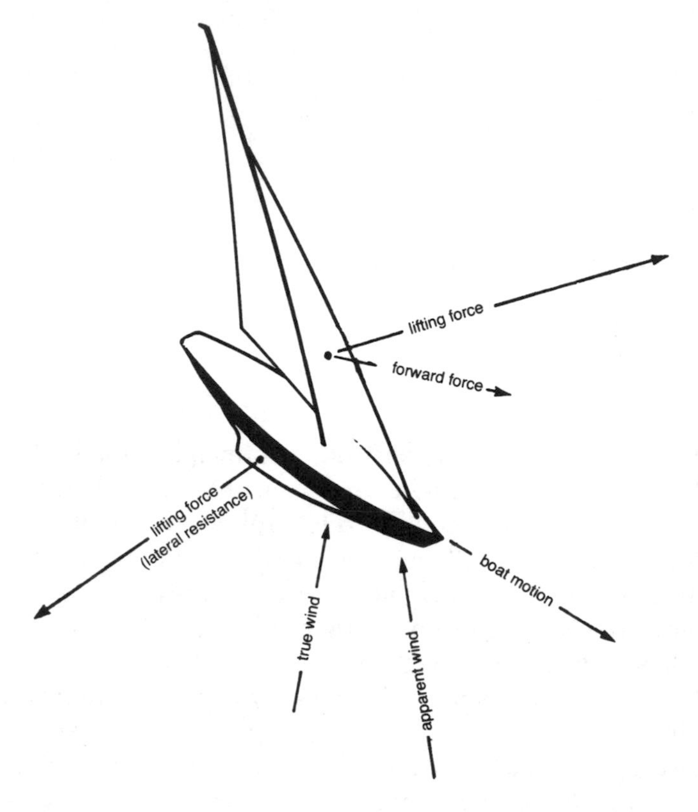

Figure 2.1
While on a closehauled or a reaching course, the flow of air (apparent wind) past the sails creates a lifting force acting diagonally forward. The forward component of this lifting force propels the boat. A lateral lifting force generated by the flow of water past the keel and underbody of the boat opposes the lateral component of the lifting force produced by the sails.

As far as a sail is concerned, the strength and direction of the TRUE WIND—the wind blowing past an anchored bell buoy for example—is completely irrelevant. All that matters is the APPARENT WIND—wind consisting of a combination of the true wind and the forward motion of the boat.

Boat motion is itself a combination of self-propelled motion and water movement or current.

Beneath the surface of the water, the keel and rudder are exact analogs of the sails—flow diverters designed to generate a lifting force in the lateral direction. The side force created by the movement of these fins through the water counterbalances the lateral component of the lifting force produced by the sails, thus enabling the sailboat to move almost directly forward.

Experience and common sense tell us that lifting forces are not the only forces affecting a moving sailboat. Drag forces, which escalate monstrously with increasing speed, retard the boat's forward progress. Whenever a boat is sailing at a constant speed, the backward component of the drag forces acting on the rig and hull precisely counterbalances the forward component of the lifting forces generated by its sails.

How are these lifting forces and drag forces created? To properly answer this central question requires a closer look at how moving fluids (including both air and water) behave when they encounter objects in their paths. We'll begin with a look at drag forces, because they are easier to understand and because the origins of lifting forces are closely related.

SKIN FRICTION AND PRESSURE DRAG

Drag, or resistance to flow, is generated in two quite different ways. The first, more obvious type of drag is SKIN FRICTION or VISCOUS DRAG, so-called because it is a consequence of the viscosity or resistance to sheer of a particular fluid. Because fluids vary enormously in their viscosity, some create far more viscous drag than others. Air is about

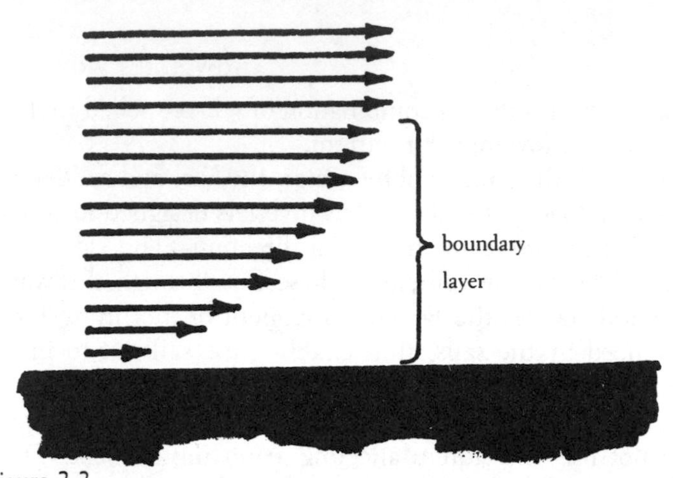

Figure 2.2
The boundary layer is a zone of slow-moving fluid close to the surface of an object. Adhesion between the surface and the fluid, as well as friction within the moving fluid causes it to form.

five times less viscous than water, and tar is hundreds of times more viscous than either.

Viscous drag occurs because, as fluid flows around an obstruction, a film of fluid molecules adhere to the surface of the object and cease to move with the flow. Fluid molecules progressively further from the surface are retarded less and less, until a point is reached where flow is unimpeded (Figure 2.2). The thickness of the BOUNDARY LAYER, in which flow is to some extent retarded by viscous forces, varies considerably depending upon the kind of fluid, flow speed and the shape and size of the object. All else being equal, a thicker boundary layer is associated with a modest increase in drag.

Roughness and irregularities on the surface of an object have little or no effect upon its drag provided they are small enough to be buried comfortably within its boundary layer. Under most sailing conditions, the boundary layer on sail surfaces is thick enough to cover seam laps, stitching, and other such minor irregularities. Furthermore, as we shall see, there are much more damaging sources of drag.

PRESSURE DRAG is a bit more complicated than skin friction. Understanding it involves not only a conceptual grasp of boundary layer behavior as just described, but also of the special relationship between flow speed and fluid pressure.

Daniel Bernoulli, in 1738, first recognized how changes in flow velocity were related to pressure changes within a moving body of fluid: increased flow velocity results in decreased pressure and vice versa. The proper explanation of this apparent paradox is a fundamental physical principle called the law of energy conservation, and goes something like this: (Hold onto your hats!) Since the total energy content of a mass of moving fluid must remain constant, any change in kinetic energy caused by acceleration or deceleration of flow must be counterbalanced by a proportional and opposite change in the potential energy content of the fluid which is manifested, in part, as pressure.

For most of us, it's easier to think of Bernoulli's principle in terms of an analogy to traffic flow on a highway (Figure 2.3). If a line of automobiles travelling single file down a paved highway at 100 km/hr encounters a construction zone and slows to 40 km/hr, each car will close on the one ahead—the traffic will "compress." At the end of the construction zone, the gap between vehicles will open again as each car accelerates away from the one behind it. This analogy can be misleading because most fluids, including air at normal sailing speeds, are incompressible; the average spacing between molecules—and hence the density of these fluids—does not vary when the flow speed changes. On the other hand, the analogy makes it easy to identify the pressure changes that actually take place as fluids flow around obstructions.

Getting back to pressure drag: when fluid particles (or molecules if you prefer) approach an obstruction in the

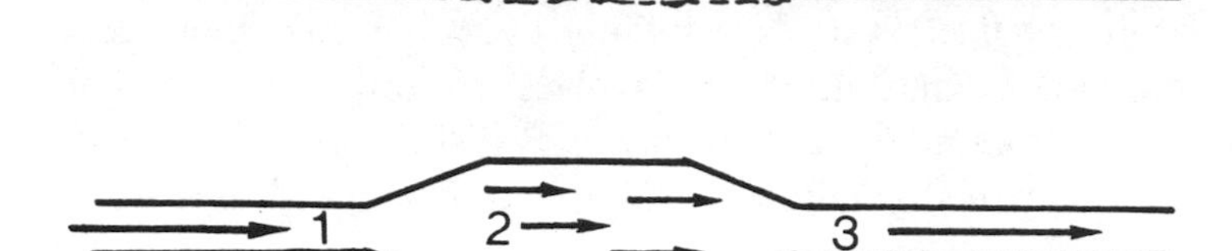

Figure 2.3
Automotive traffic flow (top diagram) provides an analogy to Bernoulli's principle. When a fast-moving line of vehicles encounters a bad stretch of roadway, each slows down, causing the line of vehicles to become compressed. The dilation of the pipe (in the lower diagram) causes the flow rate to drop as fluid progresses from 1 to 2. Moving from 2 to 3 it accelerates again. Accordingly, fluid pressure is lower at 2 than at either 1 or 3.

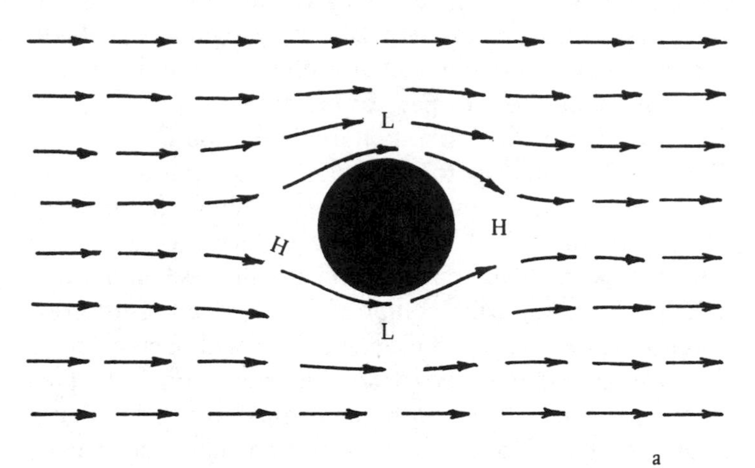

Figure 2.4
The origins of pressure drag. Longer arrows signify faster flow accompanied by lower pressure. As fluid passes around an obstruction, low pressure zones (L) form at the flanks of the object while high pressure regions are found near the upstream and downstream faces of the object where fluid is moving slowly (diagram a). Flow within the boundary layer (diagram b) is augmented between 1 and 2 by the high-to-low pressure

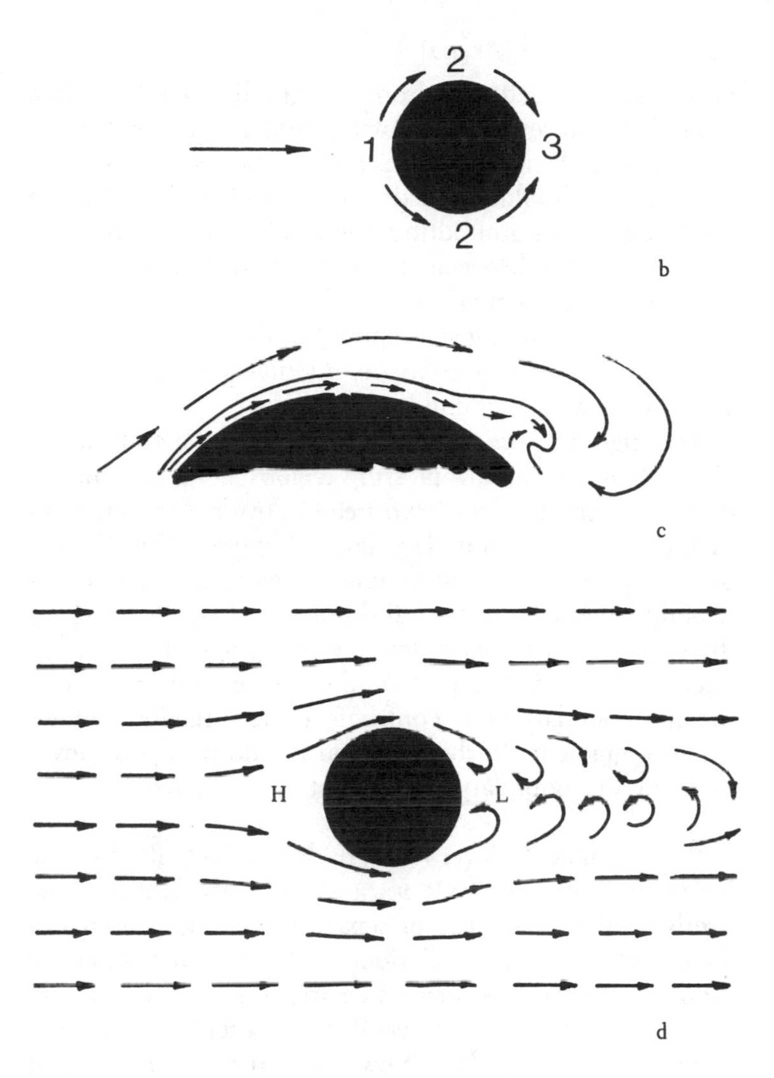

gradient, but retarded between 2 and 3 as pressure builds from low to high. A stall (diagram c) results when flow within the boundary layer stops or reverses, causing a fluid dam to form. Pressure within the wake created downstream of a boundary layer stall is lower than at the upstream face of the obstruction (diagram d). A front-to-back drag force results.

flow, they are deflected from straight line paths to pass around it. However, the moving fluid in the free stream flow off to each side of the obstruction has momentum and resists being shouldered aside. As a result, the fluid being displaced to pass around the object is squeezed through a constricted zone between the obstruction itself and a surrounding fluid "barrier" (Figure 2.4a). To pass through a constricted area in a given amount of time, the fluid must speed up. When it does so, its internal pressure drops in accordance with Bernoulli's principle.

The high pressure zones that develop at the ends of our obstruction and the low pressure regions along its flanks in between affect the slow downstream movement of the fluid in the underlying boundary layer (Figure 2.4b). On the upstream side of the obstruction, the boundary layer oozes steadily downstream over the surface, helped along by the superimposed high-to-low pressure gradient. However, once past the widest part of the obstruction, the slow-moving boundary layer confronts an adverse, low-to-high pressure gradient. In this situation the downstream movement of the boundary layer is retarded, halted, or even reversed.

When boundary layer flow grinds to a halt, fluid in the boundary layer piles up to form a temporary dam, causing overlying flow to deviate or separate from the contours of the object (Figure 2.4c). Periodically, the stagnated mass of fluid near the surface breaks free and tumbles away wreaking havoc with a smooth overall flow pattern. Stoppage or reversal of boundary layer flow is called a STALL—a most appropriate term if you think about it.

Now at last we're ready to see how pressure drag comes about. In the turbulent, tumbling WAKE downstream of a boundary layer stall, fluid particles follow long, looping paths at fairly high speeds, causing the pressure in the wake to remain quite low in accordance with Bernoulli's principle (Figure 2.4d). With high pressure at the upstream face of our object and lower pressure on the downstream side, the force we call pressure drag is generated in the downstream direction. On sails operating at normal wind speeds, the pressure drag induced by a fully developed stall is overwhelmingly greater than skin friction.

THE ORIGIN OF LIFTING FORCES

Lift is generated whenever fluid flows past an asymmetrical object because more fluid will be diverted to one side than the other (Figure 2.5 top). The side that receives the greater volume experiences faster flow, hence lower pressure (Bernoulli again). The resulting pressure gradient creates a force acting from the high pressure side toward the low pressure one.

If an object is properly shaped and oriented, so much fluid will be diverted over the high speed/low pressure side that the speed of the small amount of fluid still passing the opposite flank will drop below free stream velocity which in turn will cause a high pressure zone to form there (Figure 2.5 bottom). The uneven division of flow is further encouraged by the natural tendency of approaching fluid particles to be repelled by this high pressure zone while at the same time drawn toward the low pressure region on the opposite side. The resulting diversion of approaching fluid before it even reaches the obstruction is called UPWASH. The corresponding opposite deflection of the streamlines leaving the trailing edge of a good lifting shape is called DOWNWASH. As we have seen in Chapter 1 (Figure 1.7) upwash and downwash affect the way multiple sails in a single rig work together. When two or more boats are sailing in close company, they create the safe leeward positions and backwind zones so familiar to racing sailors (Figure 2.6).

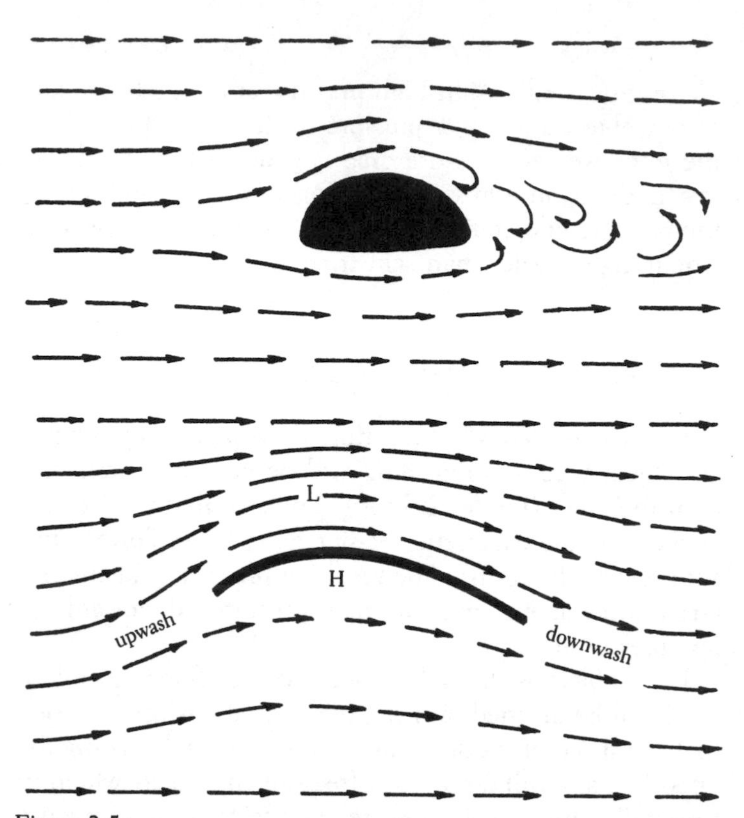

Figure 2.5
Lift is created whenever fluid flows around an asymmetrical object (top diagram) because more flow is diverted to one side (in this case the upper one), causing an unequal drop in pressure. An appropriately shaped asymmetrical object (lower diagram) will divert so much fluid to the low pressure side that the residual flow over the opposite side will be slower than free stream, and the pressure there correspondingly higher. Upwash and downwash are terms describing the deflection of fluid as it first approaches and later leaves the vicinity of a lift generating object.

DRAG AS A BYPRODUCT OF LIFT

Unfortunately, reshaping an object so that it will generate more lift when exposed to flow ordinarily causes pres-

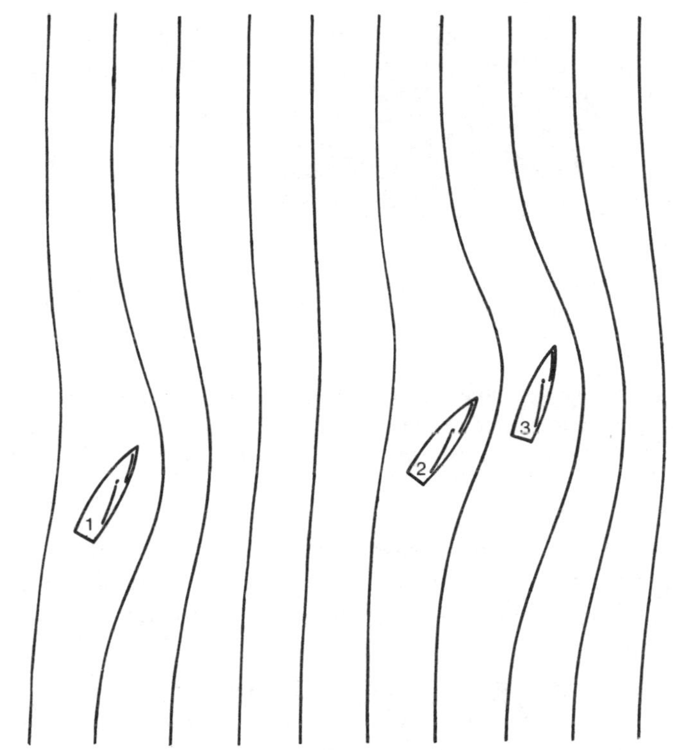

Figure 2.6
Boat 1 sailing upwind in isolation creates less upwash and downwash than the two together in close quarters. Thanks to the additional upwash provided by boat 2, boat 3 is temporarily able to point higher than boat 1. However, boat 2's pointing suffers because she is situated in the downwash created by boat 3. Boat 3 occupies a safe leeward position, and boat 2 is said to be backwinded.

sure drag to increase. This additional resistance is called INDUCED DRAG, drag associated with the production of lift. In most cases, induced drag is the most significant source of flow resistance in a properly trimmed sail.

Induced drag in sails stems from two sources. The first is a peculiarity in the way air flows around thin airfoil shapes (as opposed to thick sections such as are used for most

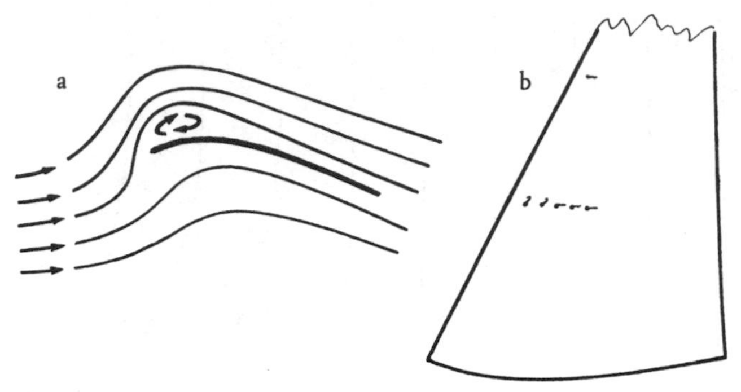

Figure 2.7
A leading edge separation bubble is created if the upwash is unable to turn tightly enough around the luff of a sail (a). A horizontal line of telltales (b) helps to detect the presence and extent of leading edge separation.

aircraft wings). As the upwash carries air from ahead and to windward of a sail over its leeward side, some of the air fairly close to the sail's surface is forced to turn abruptly around the luff of the sail. In many cases, the air is unable to negotiate so tight a turn and a LEADING EDGE SEPARATION BUBBLE forms (Figure 2.7a). The separation bubble just behind the luff of a real sail can be envisioned as an elliptical, rotating tube of entrapped air. The energy required to create and maintain a separation bubble is, of course, sapped from the surrounding flow.

Normally, the air flowing over a leeward separation bubble reattaches to the leeward surface of the sail well before it gets to the leech. However, if the sail is sheeted too tightly, or if the helmsman bears off too much without having the sheets eased, the separation bubble, which is also known as a leading edge stall, can grow into a gross "killer" stall. To verify the existence and determine the size of the leeward separation bubble, a horizontal row of small yarn TELLTALES can be attached about ten cm. apart across the girth of a sail (Figure 2.7b).

The second, more serious form of induced drag is caused by fluid moving laterally over the sides and around the ends of a three-dimensional lifting shape. It is practically impossible to prevent air from bleeding from the high pressure windward side of a sail to the low pressure leeward side, looping up and over the leech or down and under the foot in the process. This transverse air movement creates TIP VORTICES which stream continuously away from the head and foot of the sail, absorbing large amounts of energy in the process (Figure 2.8).

The amount of induced drag created by vortex shedding varies dramatically with the design features of sails and sail-

Figure 2.8
The main sources of induced drag are tip vortices caused by high pressure air on the windward side of the sail flowing over the leech and under the foot to the low pressure leeward side.

ing rigs—features such as sail profile shape (outline shape), camber distribution, and twist. These characteristics will be discussed in Chapters 3 and 4.

INTERACTIONS BETWEEN SAILS

All sailboats except catboats set more than one sail simultaneously. The way that air passes around each sail in a combination differs substantially from flow pattern that would be generated by the same sails set individually.

Figure 2.9 illustrates, better than words, how air flow around each sail in a sloop rig is influenced by its counterpart. As far as the headsail is concerned, the high speed/low pressure flow over the leeward side of the mainsail tends to suck air off the headsail leech, increasing the flow rate over the leeward face of the headsail. Faster flow over the lee side of the headsail means lower pressure in that area, which in turn causes a stronger upwash (i.e. a larger proportion of the approaching air is drawn to the leeward side of the headsail). Since the headsail is also situated in the upwash zone created by the mainsail, the angle of the air flow approaching its luff is altered substantially more than would be the case if the mainsail were absent. The more pronounced upwash represents a localized lift, permitting the boat to point higher before the headsail luffs.

Each of these effects of the mainsail leads to an increase in the lifting force generated by the headsail. Unfortunately, the headsail has the opposite effect upon the performance of the main. The forward lee face of the mainsail—the region where maximum flow speed and minimum pressure is normally generated—is immersed in the slow moving air passing the windward side of the headsail. Consequently, air flow over the leeward side of the mainsail is retarded, and the low pressure zone on the lee

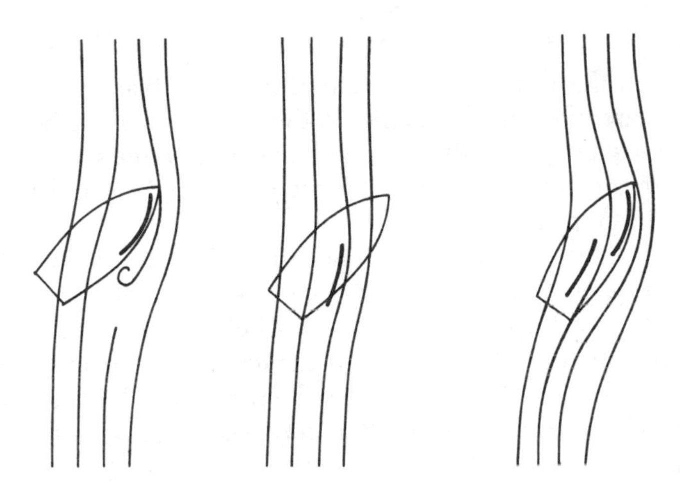

Figure 2.9
A headsail working in isolation (left) produces less upwash than the same headsail set in combination with a main (right). Consequently, the boat sailing under headsail alone cannot point as high as one with both sails set because the headsail luffs earlier. With the addition of a mainsail, a fuller headsail can be used without stalling because the low pressure zone on the windward side of the main helps to draw the air off the leeward side of the headsail before flow can stagnate there.

A mainsail working in isolation (middle) need not be sheeted nearly as far inboard as one situated in the downwash of a headsail. In practice, however, a sloop sailing under main alone cannot point effectively because the sail is too small, too flat, and suffers excessively from mast induced turbulence.

side of the main is weakened. In fact, if the windward side of the headsail is brought too close to the forward lee face of the mainsail, the pressure difference between opposite sides of the main can be reduced to zero or reversed. This causes the front of the mainsail to flutter or billow to windward and is called BACKWINDING. Contrary to popular opinion, air flows quite slowly through the slot between headsail and main, not nearly as rapidly as it moves over the forward lee side of the headsail.

Since the mainsail is situated in the downwash zone

behind the headsail, it must be sheeted so that its chord lines are more nearly parallel to the centerline of the boat. Consequently, the lifting forces it generates while sailing to windward are often almost directly abeam and of no direct use in propelling the boat.

Of course, we are not concerned with the individual efficiencies of the various sails in a rig—only with the total lift and total drag of the rig as a whole. In general, that compound or slotted rigs can generate more lift relative to the sail area employed than even the most refined single sail rigs. *However, the ratio of lift to drag tends to be less advantageous.*

For upwind sailing and close reaching, a high lift/drag ratio is extremely important because aerodynamic drag in the sails and rigging directly impedes the forward progress of the boat. For this reason sophisticated una rigs provide the very best upwind performances, and sloops are better than yawls.

On beam reaches, however, aerodynamic drag is less harmful because it acts athwartships, heeling the boat, but not retarding it directly. Here the high gross lift characteristics of compound rigs are an asset. Yawls and ketches excel on reaches, and racing sloops turn themselves into multi-slotted cutters with the addition of staysails.

3 Selecting Appropriate Sail Shapes

SAILBOAT development has progressed more slowly than aircraft development because the military and commercial applications of airplanes have justified enormous expenditures of both money and engineering talent. As a result, after only about eighty years of study, the aerodynamic behavior of aircraft wings is understood far better than that of sails, despite many centuries of sailing experience. Unfortunately, little of the knowledge gleaned from aircraft investigations can be applied to sailboats, partly because most aircraft operate at steady, high speeds, and partly because sails, unlike almost all aircraft wings, are thin, flexible cambered surfaces rather than thick rigid ones.

There are four reasons why almost all sailboats use thin, flexible sails (and will almost certainly continue to do so in the foreseeable future). First, sailboats are highly intolerant of weight high above decks. Most have very limited stability with which to counterbalance the lateral forces generated while sailing closehauled and on reaches. Weight in the rigging also increases the tendency of a boat to roll and pitch in a seaway. This is not only uncomfortable, but extremely detrimental to sailing efficiency because radical fluctuations in the direction and strength of the apparent wind are induced as the rig swings about. In most cases, rig weight so seriously erodes a sailboat's performance that it pays to save weight there even at the expense of some aerodynamic efficiency. It is unlikely that rigid wing sails will ever approach the low weight of conventional sailing rigs of the same area.

Second, thin, flexible sails can be conveniently hoisted, doused, and stowed below decks. Since sail handling operations must often be performed under difficult and even hazardous conditions, anything that makes the task easier is probably worthwhile. In contrast, rigid wing sails are difficult to de-power in strong winds. When not in use, they must either be unstepped or dismantled to prevent the moored boat from sailing around uncontrollably whenever a stiff wind blows.

A third advantage of thin, flexible sails is their low cost—at least in comparison with delicate, sophisticated structures like wing sails. The basic economy of the flexible, fabric sail becomes strikingly evident when contrasted to the cost of its alternatives; aircraft owners can vouch for the high price of airframe maintenance.

Finally, thin, cambered sails actually perform better than wing sails of the same area at low wind speeds. Since sailboats travel quite slowly, and operate a good part of the time with little apparent wind, this is a significant asset.

Since thin, flexible sails are the only reasonable choice for most wet sailing applications, how should a sailor or sailmaker go about selecting the most suitable shapes or curvatures? Without access to the expensive laboratory testing procedures employed by aircraft engineers, the best available test bed for sail shapes is the sport of sailboat racing. Empirical trial and error race course development, particularly in one design and level classes, has taught us most of what we know about good sail shapes, for both racing boats and cruisers. In recent years particularly, since the use of yarn telltales to detect flow patterns close to sail surfaces has become popular, the fine tuning of sail shapes has progressed rapidly.

OPTIMIZING LIFT/DRAG RATIOS

The most demanding test of sail shape is upwind sailing, because the lifting force generated by a closehauled sail is directed mostly sideways (Figure 3.1). The lateral component of the lifting force heels the yacht, but does nothing to promote forward progress. To make matters worse, aero-

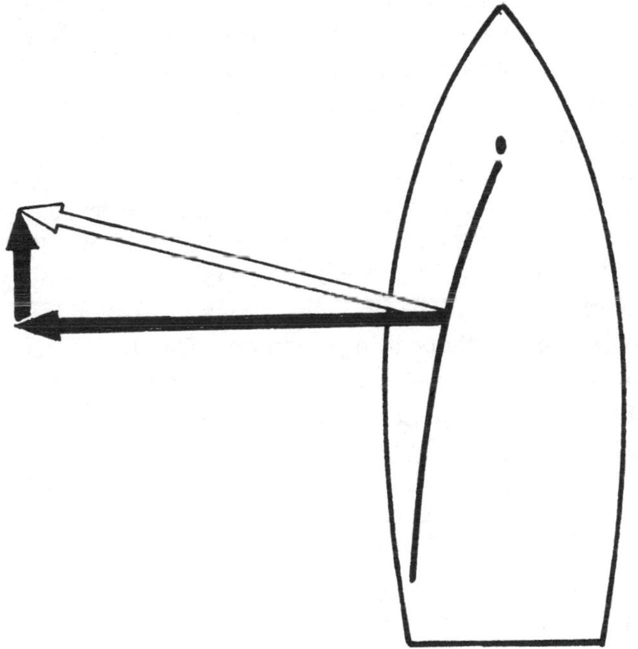

Figure 3.1
The net lifting force created by a closehauled sail (white arrow) can be resolved into a large lateral component and a small forward one.

dynamic drag forces on a closehauled sail act diagonally backward—counter to the desired direction of motion.

Lift/drag ratio, as mentioned in the preceding chapter, is the most important determinant of the real-life windward success of a particular sail set on a particular boat. It is quite possible, even easy, to go to windward more slowly using a powerful high lift sail with excessively high drag characteristics than by using a more suitably shaped sail that produces less lift. This can happen even when the wind is gentle enough to prevent the former sail from overpowering the boat.

Of course, not all sailing is upwind work (even if it often seems so). As we have already seen, aerodynamic drag does little harm on a beam reaching course, where its main effect is to heel the boat rather than to directly retard it. On broad reaches, and before the wind, aerodynamic drag is a major propulsive force in its own right.

The lift-generating ability of a sail, as well as its lift/drag ratio under a variety of wind conditions, is determined by its size, its three-dimensional shape, and the environment in which it operates. Four types of variables have proved particularly important: camber and camber distribution; twist; profile shape; and operating environment—the influence of nearby sails, the boat's hull, and the water's surface. Let's examine these areas in light of on-the-water sail testing experience.

CAMBER AND CAMBER DISTRIBUTION

In Chapter 1, I described how the three-dimensional shape of a sail can be pictured as a stack of cambered shapes, each with its own depth/chord ratio and maximum depth location. It has been shown, time and time again, that variations in sail camber of less than 1 percent have major effects upon yacht performance. Without a great deal of practice, most people find it impossible to judge the camber of a sail with sufficient accuracy to be of much use. The proper method of evaluating sail camber and camber distribution is with photographs.

Taking useful sail photographs is quite easy. A fast black and white film should be used to permit both a reasonably short exposure (less than 1/100 sec.) and a small aperture (preferably f16 or f22) for maximum depth of field. A wide angle lens (ideally 28 mm focal length for a 35 mm camera) gives the best results, but a normal lens is OK. The camera should be positioned low to deck, at the center of the foot, and as close to the sail surface as possible. To attain this position while photographing headsails, the photographer should lie on the foredeck close to the leeward rail. For mainsails, the companionway or cabin top usually provides a satisfactory, and somewhat more comfortable, vantage point.

After the photographs are printed, the camber at various heights can be measured by drawing the chord across a seam or draft stripe and measuring maximum depth and maximum depth location with a scale ruler (Figure 3.2). Contrasting DRAFT STRIPES, which can even be drawn on the sail with a Magic Marker, give the best results, but reasonable camber estimates can be made using horizontal seams. However, with vertical paneled sails, draft stripes are a necessity in order to evaluate camber either with a camera or by direct observation (Figure 3.3).

Depth/chord ratios of almost all sails fall in the range of 11 percent to 19 percent. Only some spinnakers are built fuller. Maximum depth positions usually vary from about 38 percent aft to 47 percent aft. Figure 3.4 diagrams the normal spectrum of sail cambers.

It has been firmly established that light and medium air

Figure 3.2
Even if a crosscut sail lacks contrasting draft strips, a sail photograph can be used to evaluate camber. This genoa has a depth/chord ratio of 18 percent and its maximum depth is located 46 percent aft.

Figure 3.3
The camber of vertical cut sails can be evaluated only if draft stripes are provided. Here the depth/chord ratio at the top stripe is 17 percent and maximum depth is 47 percent aft.

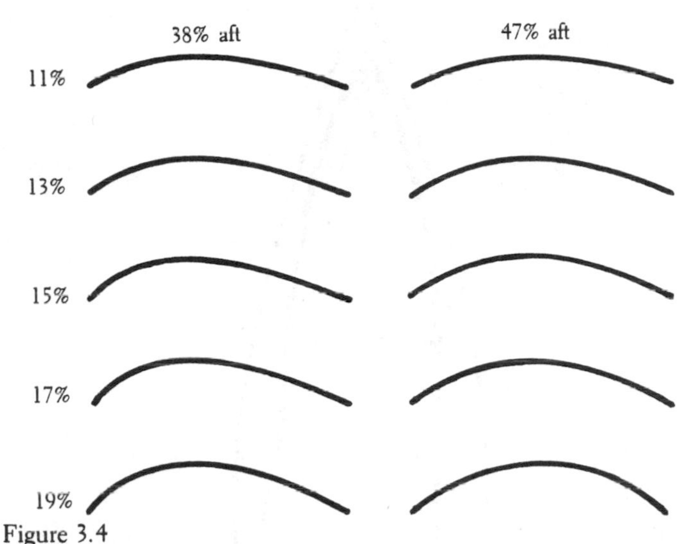

Figure 3.4
Sail cambers normally range from 11 percent (flat) to 19 percent (full). Maximum depth locations range from 38 percent (draft forward) to 47 percent (draft aft).

sails, such as the #1 genoas of sloops, work best if the camber increases gradually toward the head. Good depth/chord ratios at the ¼, ½, and ¾ levels of an all-purpose genoa for a contemporary thirty-five-foot ocean racing boat are about 15 percent, 16½ percent, and 17½ percent respectively. Curiously enough, the optimum depth/chord ratios for a light #1 in six knots apparent wind and a heavy #1 in twenty knots are quite similar, although these sails must be constructed very differently to compensate for obvious differences in headstay sag and fabric loading.

In general, boats with small keels, inefficiently shaped keels, exceptionally easily driven hulls, or relatively low stability all perform better with genoas that are 1 percent to 2 percent flatter than the norm described above.

Modern #2 genoas are slightly flatter than #1s (14 percent near the foot and 15 percent toward the head are typical figures), but the LP measurement, and hence the

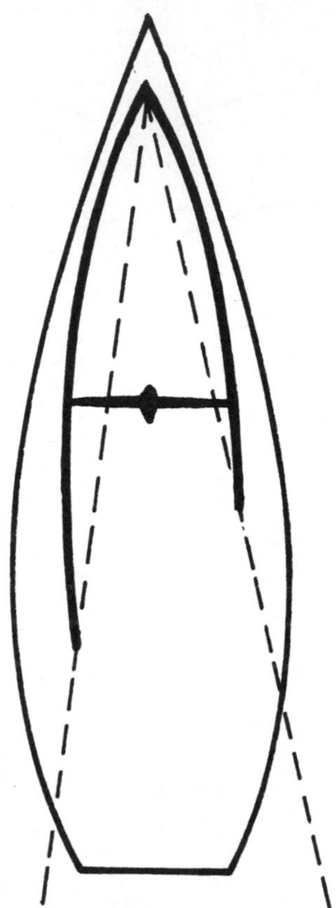

Figure 3.5
A #1 genoa (shown on the port side) can be used with a smaller sheeting angle than a #2 genoa (starboard side) because it wraps around spreader(s) to a greater extent.

actual depth of the sail, is significantly reduced. The reduced girth of #2 genoas and lappers makes it difficult or impossible to sheet these sails to a small enough angle (as viewed from above), because the leech area tends to contact the spreaders (Figure 3.5). In contrast, a #1 genoa overlaps the mast sufficiently to effectively wrap around the spreaders. Because of this stumbling block, #2 genoas are often built a little flatter than would otherwise be optimal to prevent the pointing ability of the yacht from being excessively compromised. (See the discussion of entry angle in the following section.)

Modern #3 and #4 headsails generally have an average camber around 14 percent, although a tendency toward fuller sails has been evident in recent years. Since these sails do not overlap the mast, they can be sheeted as far inboard as desired, and a full shape often seems to help drive a boat through the waves that accompany strong winds in most areas.

Mainsails on boats with headsails must be flatter than genoas because they are situated in the downwash of the sail ahead. Typical depth/chord ratios for a good mainsail on a masthead sloop might be 12 percent at the ¼ height, 13 percent at the ½ height, and 14 percent at the ¾ level, but sailmakers and sailors are much farther from a consensus here than in regard to headsail camber. On modern racing boats and increasing numbers of cruising boats the camber and camber distribution of the mainsail can be altered radically while under way, and good racing crews do so almost constantly.

Mizzens are situated in the combined downwash of the headsail and main. As mentioned in Chapter 1, they must be board flat to work at all while sailing upwind. In terms of camber ratio, this means depth/chord ratios under 10 percent.

MAXIMUM DEPTH LOCATION AND ENTRY ANGLE

The position of maximum depth is just one characteristic of the cambered shape of a sail at each height, but it is important enough to warrant special attention. Maximum depth location to a large extent determines the shape of the luff region, which in turn has a major effect upon the aerodynamic behavior of the entire sail.

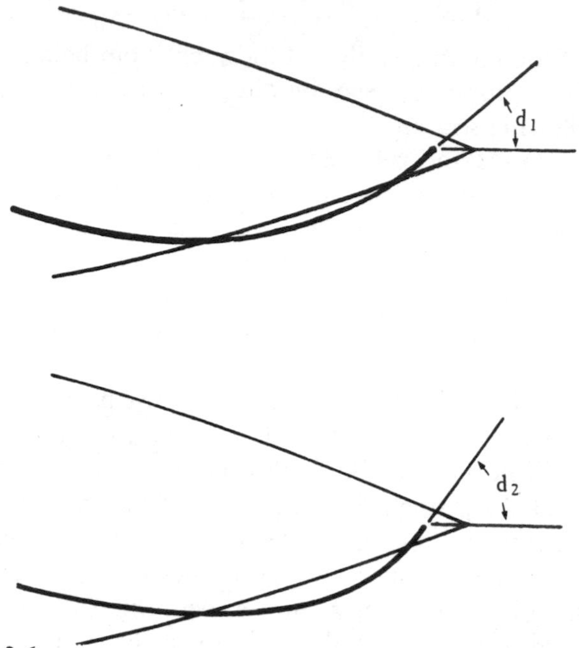

Figure 3.6
All else being equal, a draft aft sail (top) has a smaller entry angle than a draft forward one (bottom).

An important characteristic of any sail, and particularly of a headsail, is its ENTRY ANGLE—the angle between the leading edge of the sail as it is trimmed on the boat and the boat's center line. Smaller entry angles can permit higher pointing provided lift/drag ratios of sails and keel are equal to the task. Obviously, if camber and trim remain the same in other respects, a sail with its maximum draft further aft will have a smaller entry angle (Figure 3.6).

In general, a well-shaped, properly trimmed sail will luff uniformly along the entire length of its luff. This occurs only when the entry angles at every level in the sail are correct with respect to one another. This does not mean that the entry angle should be the same at all levels; the amount of upwash induced in the approaching airstream as well as the angle of the apparent wind changes progressively as one moves up or down a sailing rig. However, if a glance up the luff of a headsail reveals that the entry angle changes radically or fluctuates, you can anticipate less than optimal performance. A series of three or more pairs of yarn telltales approximately 15 cm (6″) long and 35 to 45 cm (14 to 18″) aft of the luff are the best test of entry uniformity. If all luff simultaneously, the entry angles are essentially correct (Figure 3.7).

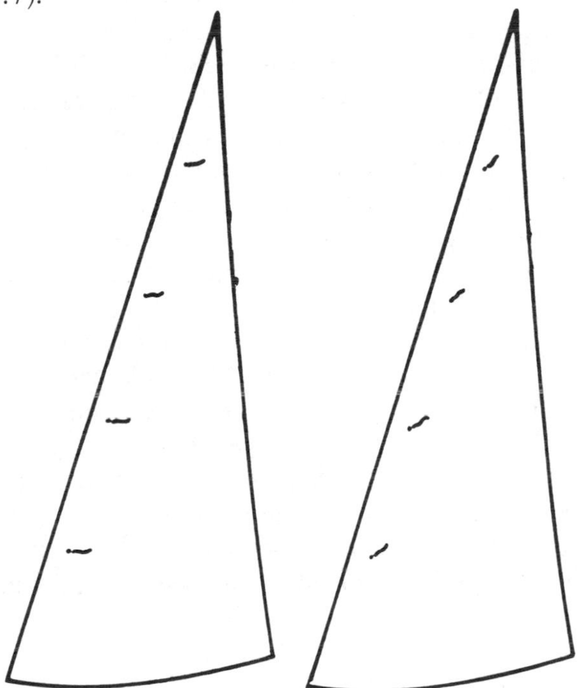

Figure 3.7
A series of telltales positioned at several heights along the luff of a headsail will show whether the entry angles at these different heights are in balance with one another (left). All the windward telltales lift simultaneously when the helmsman luffs up (right).

Draft aft, small entry angle sails have some drawbacks. Draft forward headsails—those with maximum depth locations less than 42 percent aft—will tolerate larger variations in angle of attack (defined as the angle of a sail's chord to the apparent wind) without losing too much lift. For this reason, heavy weather sails which are used in conditions where rough water makes accurate steering difficult or impossible should be more draft forward than light air sails. In heavy weather, too, the ratio of wind speed to boat speed is higher, causing the apparent wind to be further aft, and making a fine entry angle less of a necessity for satisfactory pointing.

Modern genoas for light winds and smooth waters are quite draft aft—generally 45 percent to 48 percent. However, expert sailors all seem to agree that headsails whose maximum draft strays aft of 50 percent are slow—their drag is disproportionately high relative to the lift they produce. Apparently the pronounced curvature in the aft portions of very draft aft sails makes them prone to major stalls as described in Chapter 2.

Optimal maximum depth locations for mainsails are also generally almost 50 percent aft. Mainsails with the draft further forward tend to suffer excessive backwinding, particularly when used with large overlap genoas. Of course mainsails with maximum depth locations near 50 percent have considerable curvature near the leech and are quite prone to stalls and flow separation aft. For this reason it has become conventional to attach telltales to the mainsail leech.

TWIST

Unless the air is still, it is physically impossible to trim a sail made of flexible material so that the chord lines at different heights all fall on the same plane. Lifting forces

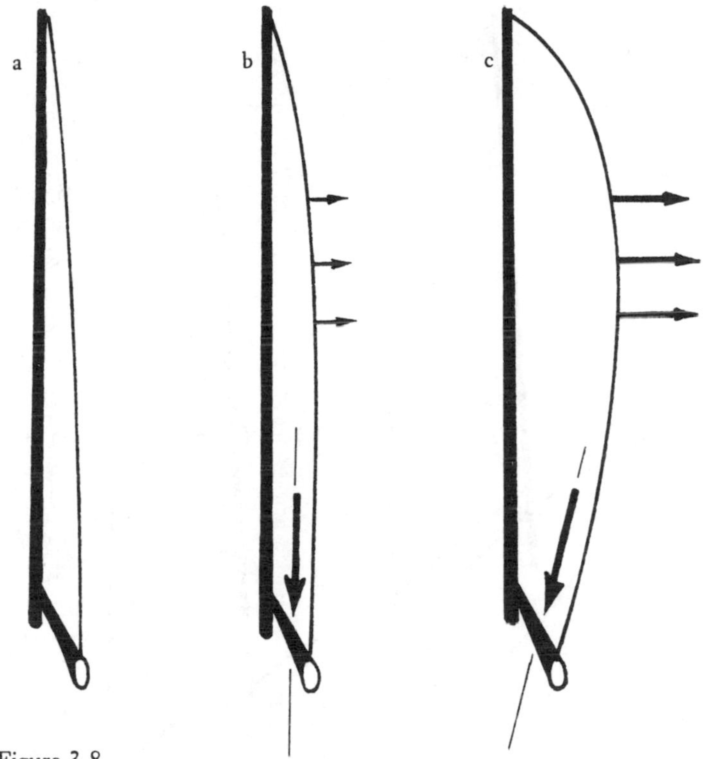

Figure 3.8
The chords at all heights in a sail will fall on a flat plane only when there is no wind (diagram a). As soon as even a gentle side force is generated (small arrows in b), the upper portions of the sail twist off to leeward, inducing comparatively large stresses in the sailcloth near the leech (large arrow in b). More wind causes larger side forces and more lateral deflection of the upper leech (diagram c). Because the sail is now twisted more, the sailcloth of the lower leech is angled more appropriately to resist these side forces, and stress on the sailcloth may increase only moderately.

generated by the top portion of the sail inevitably cause it to bend off to leeward until tension in the sail fabric itself counterbalances the lateral load (Figure 3.8). In essence, the lower portions of a flexible sail act like a broad, flat main sheet to trim the upper parts. The progressive increase in

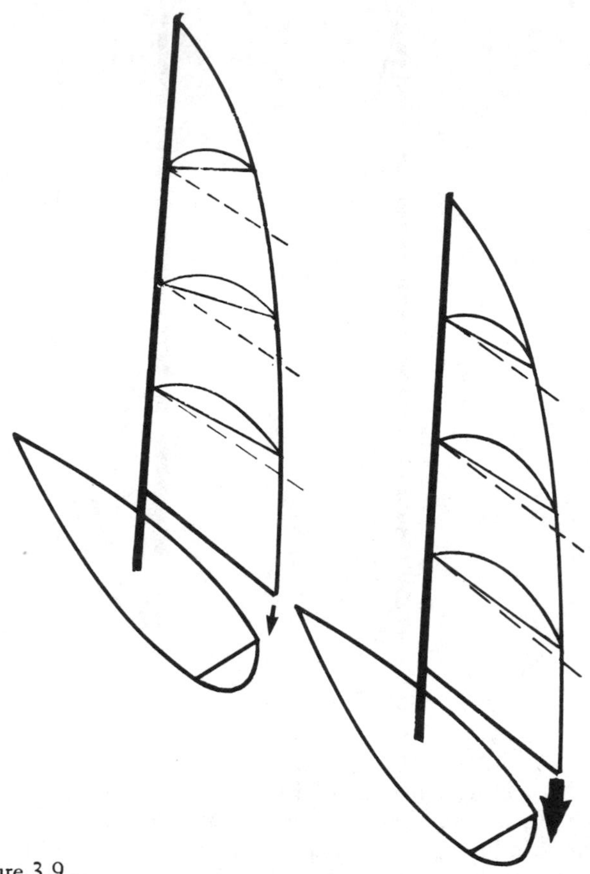

Figure 3.9
By increasing the downward pull on the clew, a highly twisted sail (left) can be changed into a less twisted one with more camber in the leech area (right).

the angles made by the chord lines of the sail at greater heights in the sail is called TWIST.

Fortunately, triangular sails actually perform best with significant and generally achievable amounts of twist. Exactly how much depends upon camber, the shape of the sail in profile, and the configuration of the rig as a whole.

When a sail is trimmed for less twist by increasing the leech tension or downward force applied to the clew, the camber of the sail will simultaneously increase and the maximum depth location will move aft, particularly toward the top of the sail (Figure 3.9). This makes good sense if you think about it. First, more leech tension preloads the sail fabric so sidewise lifting forces are counterbalanced before quite so much lateral deflection has occurred. Second, when the top portions of the leech bend away to leeward less, the leech area contributes an increased proportion of the total camber of the sail. Naturally, the extra camber provided by a so-called TIGHT LEECH is added to the aft portion of the sail, so not only does the total camber increase, but the maximum depth location shifts aft.

Because twist, camber, and maximum depth location are all affected by leech tension, sailmakers strive to design sails that will set more or less automatically; i.e. if the twist is right then camber and maximum depth locations will be more or less correct as well. If any of these characteristics is excessively far out of balance with respect to the others, it will be impossible to optimize sail shape using trim adjustments.

SAIL SHAPE IN PROFILE

The outlines of modern sails, although for the most part roughly triangular, vary considerably. Particularly significant is the ASPECT RATIO or height-to-girth ratio. The foot of a sail, and to some extent, the upper leech, are major efficiency drains, because in these regions high pressure air from the windward side can flow laterally around the edge to the low pressure zone on the leeward side as described in Chapter 2 (see Figure 2.8). As a result, the pressure differential across the sail is reduced and lift is lost. At the

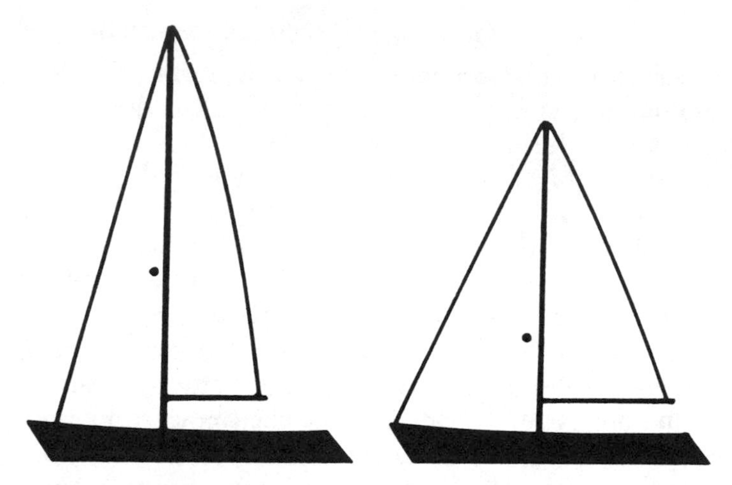

Figure 3.10
Both the aerodynamic center of effort and the center of gravity are further above deck in a high aspect rig (left) than in a low aspect rig with the same sail area (right).

same time, the special type of turbulence called a tip vortex is formed, sometimes at several places simultaneously. Energy expended in tip vortex formation represents an increase in induced drag, which you will recall is drag created as an unwanted by-product of lift production.

A high aspect sail (tall and narrow) has a smaller proportion of its total area situated close to its ends. Accordingly, its induced drag is reduced and substantially higher lift/drag ratios result. All is not roses, however. Both the center of gravity of a high aspect rig and its center of effort (average point of action for all aerodynamic forces) are further above deck than in the case of a low aspect rig (Figure 3.10). Consequently, for a given amount of lift, the boat will heel more. It is becoming apparent that when the aspect ratio of contemporary high aspect rigs are increased still further, little or no improvement in upwind performance is achieved because the lift/drag ratio improves only marginally, while the center of effort and center of gravity climb inexorably. It is therefore unlikely that we will soon see sail aspect ratios that appreciably exceed today's maximum values of approximately 4 to 1.

By preventing pressure equalization under the foot of headsails, significant increases in lift and reductions in induced drag can often be achieved. This is quite readily achieved for headsails by building the foot of the sail to contact the deck. As a result, the boat's hull acts as an end plate to prevent the air from bleeding around the sail foot. Even small gaps greatly erode the advantage of deck-sweeping headsails. A 15cm (6″) space reduces efficiency virtually as much as a gap one meter or more in width. Booms low enough to achieve a worthwhile end plate effect are dangerous and impractical, so mainsails are rarely considered as candidates for this treatment.

The drawbacks of deck-sweeping headsails are a minor tendency to chafe on lifelines etc., and a major loss of visibility forward and to leeward, especially when the sail is a large overlap genoa. The comparatively high incidence of port-starboard collisions between modern boats is almost certainly a consequence of the popularity of this route to greater aerodynamic efficiency.

SAIL COMBINATIONS

The complex interactions between the individual sails that comprise the rig of a sloop, cutter, ketch, or yawl have already been discussed at some length. At this point, I will simply repeat two main points: First, all the sails in any of these rigs interact intimately to create what is, in essence, a single lift-producing unit. Second, the camber, maximum depth location, twist, and profile of each sail in this unit affect these design features in each other sail. Some further specifics will be provided in Chapter 9 when sail trim is discussed.

SHAPE FAULTS

It is universally agreed that good sails should have smooth, continuous camber—no bumps, hollows, folds, or creases. In practice this is something of a Holy Grail—constantly sought, but almost never achieved. Indeed, minor faults in the leeches of sails without battens—hooking, fall off, or a combination of both—are so prevalent that most sailmakers regard them as virtually inevitable. Sailmakers tend to focus their attention on the overall shape of a sail, the features described earlier in this chapter, while their customers often seem somewhat more likely to concern themselves with small-scale irregularities. Expert sailors generally believe that overall shape is of dominant importance, but there is really little reliable data on the effect of small-scale shape flaws on sail performance, unless of course, they are so small as to be buried in the boundary layer.

Not all shape faults can be considered small-scale. Many if not most of the sails currently in use on the waters of the world have shapes quite unlike those described as near optimal in this chapter. The technology that has been developed to design and build sails with particular three-dimensional shapes is explained in the five chapters that follow. Using the same or related methods, sailmakers can frequently improve the shapes of existing sails, a subject I will address in Chapter 11.

4 Basic Sail Design

IN the last chapter, I discussed the three-dimensional sail shapes that have proved most effective on modern boats for close reaching and upwind work. Our next step is to look more closely at how a sailmaker proceeds when presented with the problem of creating a particular shape.

When it comes to sailing performance, the only sail shape that ultimately matters is the three-dimensional shape of the sail in actual use; its so-called FLYING SHAPE. A number of diverse factors—luff, curvature, broadseaming, fabric stretch, sail trim, and rig tune—all play a role in determining flying shape, as was explained in the first chapter. There are many different ways to vary and combine these elements that will ultimately generate the same flying sail shape, at least in one given set of sailing conditions.

Different sail design strategies do result in marked differences in on-the-water sail performance. Significantly, however, these differences are most apparent in variable wind conditions or when it is desirable to deliberately alter sail shape using trimming techniques.

A CLOSER LOOK AT THE SOURCES OF CAMBER

A fundamental rule governs the control of sail camber in both sailmaking and sail trimming situations. *Anything*

Figure 4.1
More headstay sag and less mast bend make the headsail and mainsail of the boat on the left fuller than their counterparts on the right.

which increases a chord length (luff to leech distance) will reduce the camber in that region, while anything that decreases the chord length increases it. The girths of a sail are, of course, fixed during its construction. After that (disregarding minor girth changes due to cloth stretch) any change in luff-to-leech distance must be reflected in a corresponding change in sail curvature or camber. Understanding this principle will assist enormously in appreciating how changes in sail construction and sail trim will affect flying shapes.

Consider, for example, the effect of increased headstay sag upon the camber of a headsail, or for that matter, the similar effect of reduced mast bend upon the camber of a mainsail (Figure 4.1). When either change takes place, points along the luff of the sail are moved aft, while the positions of points on the leech change very little. According to our fundamental rule, when points on the luff are brought closer to points on the leech, a sail becomes deeper. Following a similar line of reasoning, it can be seen that if one sail is designed and built with more luff round than another, otherwise identical, sail, the extra girth in the first sail will provide added camber or fullness to its flying shape.

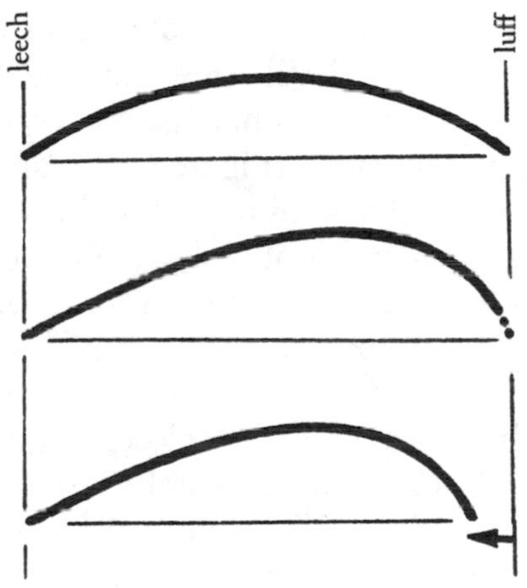

Figure 4.2
Additional luff round or girth forward (indicated by dotted section in the middle diagram) increases the camber of the sail cross section shown at the top and shifts the position of maximum depth further forward. A similar result is achieved by reducing the chord length with more headstay sag or less mast bend (bottom diagram).

Fullness added by increased luff round results in additional girth being inserted immediately behind the luff. As a result, the sail not only becomes fuller, but more draft forward as well (Figure 4.2). Similarly, if fullness is added by increasing headstay sag or reducing mast bend, the lost chord length is removed from the luff region of the sail which accordingly becomes rounder forward (Figure 4.2). Conversely, if luff round or headstay sag is decreased, or, in the case of a mainsail, if mast bend is increased, the sail becomes not only flatter but more draft aft.

The effects of changing luff curvature are most pronounced near the head of a sail because here, where the overall girth is small, a given change in girth or chord length has a proportionally larger effect.

The effects of sail trim on camber can also be predicted using our fundamental rule to relate chord length to sail girth. At the most basic level, even a perfectly flat stretch-free "tin sail" will assume camber as the leech and luff are brought closer to each other (Figure 4.3). Camber is usually introduced in the foot regions of sails in this way. By adjusting sheet lead position or outhaul, the clew can be moved physically closer to tack or further from it, causing corresponding changes in foot camber.

To demonstrate how camber can be introduced in the foot of a sail by moving the clew closer to the tack, simply grasp a sheet of paper at two adjacent corners and bend one edge into an arc. Naturally, some of the curvature you induce in that edge will be transferred into the rest of the sheet as well.

A second aspect of sail trim (the concept of twist that was introduced in the last chapter) can also be interpreted in terms of the fundamental rule. Given a constant wind velocity, a more powerful downward pull on the clew (i.e. more leech tension) will simultaneously reduce twist and

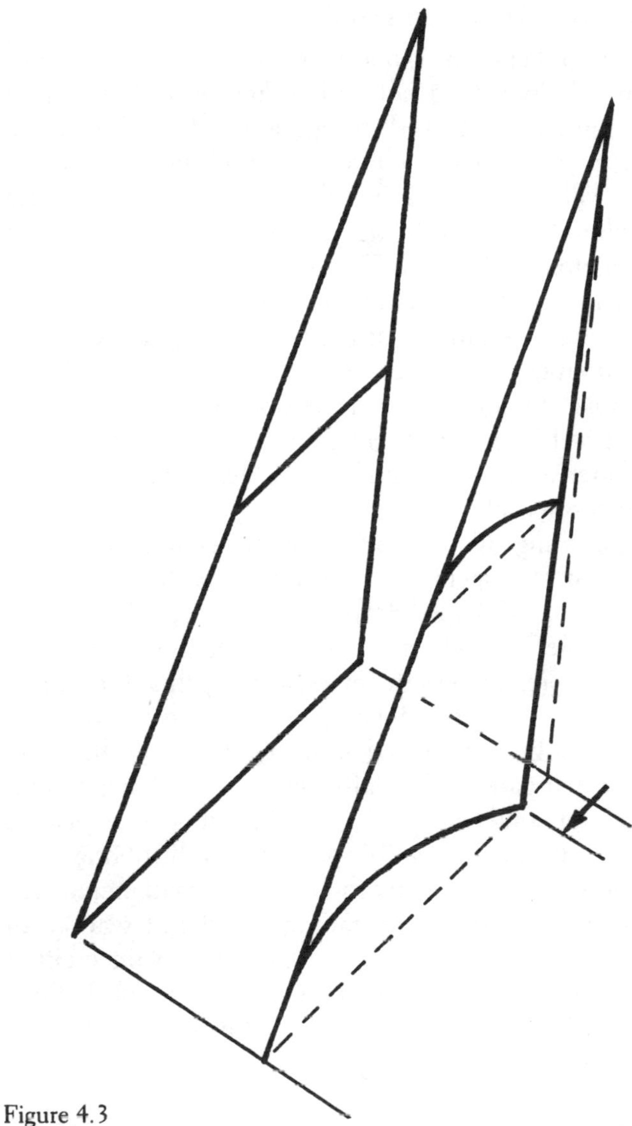

Figure 4.3
Reducing the chord length of the foot of a sail by moving the clew closer to the tack adds camber to a sail, not only at the foot but, to some extent, aloft as well.

cause the camber of the sail to increase, particularly near its head. It is helpful (and not entirely inaccurate) to picture the leech itself as a curved string that can be pulled into a closer approximation of a straight line by increased leech tension. When this is done, the string representing the leech will not only tend to sag away to leeward less, but will be forced closer to the luff. The result is shorter chords and greater camber in accordance with our fundamental rule.

Like changes in luff curvature, the effects of altered leech tension are most pronounced near the head of a sail. However, unlike the former, leech tension changes have their greatest effect in the leech area. Thus an increase in leech tension increases camber and moves the maximum depth location further aft.

Broadseaming, like the other camber generating factors discussed so far, operates in accordance with our fundamental rule of sail shape. However, most people find broadseaming easier to understand in terms of the basic beach ball analogy presented in the first chapter. Just as the doubly curved segments of a beach ball permit a more or less spherical shape to be constructed from flat stock, so the more subtly tapered panels of a sail generate a good approximation of compound curvature. Broadseaming is a versatile tool for fine tuning the camber and camber distribution of a sail because it can be added or removed in small increments wherever needed (or at any rate at the closest seam). An identical flying shape can, by and large, be obtained either by using more luff round (or alternatively, less luff hollow) in conjunction with less positive broadseaming, or the opposite combination.

MOLDED SHAPES VS. FLYING SHAPES

Broadseaming and, to some extent, luff curvature together create what some sailmakers call a MOLDED SHAPE—the shape that a sail assumes when it is hung up horizontally in the sail loft or set on an indoor horizontal test track. However, when the sail is in use, aerodynamic and trimming loads go to work to distort the molded shape into the flying shape. Part, but not all, of this distortion is a result of cloth stretch. It is important to realize that foot camber and twist are not consequences of cloth stretch; even a completely stretch-free sail would display these traits in use.

Totally stretch-free sails are an impossible dream. All materials deform somewhat under even the smallest loads. A steel reinforced concrete floor might appear perfectly rigid, but in reality it dimples slightly when even a kitten walks across it. Although it is true that some of the high tech sailcloths currently in use stretch only slightly under normal sailing loads (see Chapter 6) they are exceptional. In most cases, fabric stretch is an important determinant of flying shape.

Stretch in sails is caused both by deliberately induced trimming loads (luff and foot tension adjustments) and by aerodynamic forces. The specific effects of sail trimming adjustments upon sail shape will be explained in Chapter 9. Also, the effects of aerodynamic loading will be described in Chapter 5. For the moment, it's most important to appreciate that the primary effect of cloth stretch is to make a sail fuller.

HOW SAILS ARE DESIGNED

There are two distinct ways to approach a sail design problem. First is the traditional or empirical approach—design based upon trial and error experience. In theory, given an understanding of the basic principles governing sail shape (even just the skeletal version presented here) it would eventually be possible to design good sails simply by adjusting current attempts on the basis of previous results. Of course, a sailmaker building sails as a business cannot afford many serious errors, so good judgment, accurate evaluation of results achieved, and excellent record keeping become essential features of a viable empirical design system.

Purely analytical design represents the other end of the spectrum. Relevant characteristics of sail shape such as basic geometry, desired luff curvature, twist, and camber distributions, as well as fabric stretch characteristics, are used as a basis for attempting to predict a combination of broadseaming and luff curvature that will produce the intended result. In theory at least, a good analytical design approach can generate precisely the desired three-dimensional flying shape with every use. In practice, there are generally two principal drawbacks. First is the considerable expertise and expense involved in the necessary research and development. Second is the natural tendency for complex systems to make predictive errors, simply because so many variables are involved. To offset these drawbacks, sailmaking firms using analytical design also maintain design files, and assess each computer printout with the critical eye of experience.

A good sail design can be generated by an empirical approach, an analytical approach, or almost any combination of the two. The fact that a sailmaker has a computer doesn't mean a great deal in itself. What matters, of course, is how skilfully that computer is used.

5 Sailcloth Fundamentals

THE preceding chapter described how the all-important flying shape of a sail is controlled by four basic factors: luff curvature, bending and twisting of the sail's surface, broadseaming, and sailcloth stretch. Sailmakers often seem to spend as much time worrying about the last of these four areas—fabric deformation—as they do about the other three shape determining factors combined.

There are two reasons why sailcloth properties and particularly cloth stretch characteristics warrant particularly close attention. Firstly, the way cloth stretch typically alters sail shape in gusty winds is particularly unfortunate and difficult to counteract. If the wind increases and trim is not altered, a sail will ordinarily become somewhat fuller and more draft aft as a consequence of fabric stretch. Optimum boat performance in a rising wind would call for a flatter, more draft forward sail shape—exactly the opposite of what we get!

Secondly, there is little or nothing a sailmaker or sail user can do about the characteristics of a sailcloth once the material is purchased and incorporated in a sail (short of an outright sail replacement). The sailcloth literally is the sail. To make matters worse, selecting an appropriate cloth is not simply a matter of checking a blank on an order form. Sailcloth manufacture is as much an art as a science, and different shipments of even the same fabric routinely vary substantially from one another.

Because sailcloth characteristics are so important in determining the ultimate success of a sail, and because there is no satisfactory way to rectify an inappropriate cloth selection, it is particularly valuable for prospective sail purchasers to know something about sailcloth. This chapter begins with a look at yarn making and weaving—the early steps in the manufacture of sailcloth. It concludes with a description of key sailcloth characteristics which will provide a basis for evaluating finished fabrics.

POPULAR PLASTICS FROM BIG-TIME INDUSTRY

Virtually all modern sailcloth (except spinnaker cloth), is made wholly or largely from polyester, a synthetic fiber which is marketed under the trade name Dacron® in North America and Terelene® abroad. Spinnaker cloth is made of nylon, a plastic whose name was at one time also a trade name, but which has become a part of everyday language.

To make polyester thread, polyester resin (not unlike the resins used in fiberglass boat building) is extruded through an array of minute nozzles into a catalytic bath. The catalyst in the bath triggers a chemical reaction which turns the fluid resin into a tough, flexible solid. As the tiny strands of polyester emerge from the nozzles, they are mechanically twisted into threads, called YARNS. Nylon yarns are made by a similar process—hot, molten nylon is forced through tiny nozzles and the emerging strands are twisted together.

Incidentally, Mylar® is a trade name for catalyzed polyester in a sheet or film form. Chemically it is identical to the polyester used in Dacron® cloth. However, the long polyester molecules in a yarn are aligned to a large extent during the extrusion process whereas the molecules in a

Mylar® film are randomly oriented. As a result, polyester yarns are actually quite a bit stronger in tension for a given cross-sectional area than polyester films.

A few sailcloths contain yarns made of an aramid plastic called Kevlar®, originally developed for reinforcing cords in automobile tires. Kevlar® is dramatically stronger and more stretch resistant than polyester. However, it is also about five times more expensive and seriously vulnerable to damage from flexing and creasing.

Modern synthetic materials are generally produced by giant chemical firms. The DuPont Company was primarily responsible for the development of the products mentioned, as well as being the largest single manufacturer of them. It is important to realize that the sailcloth industry is an almost insignificantly small portion of the market for polyester, nylon, and Kevlar®. Although these materials are quite well suited to sailmaking applications, there is no reason to believe that any of them represents an ultimate solution. On the other hand, the enormous costs of research and development in the plastics industry pretty much preclude the possibility of new materials specifically or primarily for sailmaking.

SAILCLOTH WEAVING

All major North American sailcloth manufacturers are located in the eastern United States where they can subcontract weaving and finishing work to giant textile mills. The capital cost of modern textile equipment is prohibitive in view of the modest volume of material consumed by the sailcloth market.

Weaving is performed by high-speed power looms which must be set up for long runs for economical operation. To set up a loom, a parallel array of about 4,000 WARP YARNS,

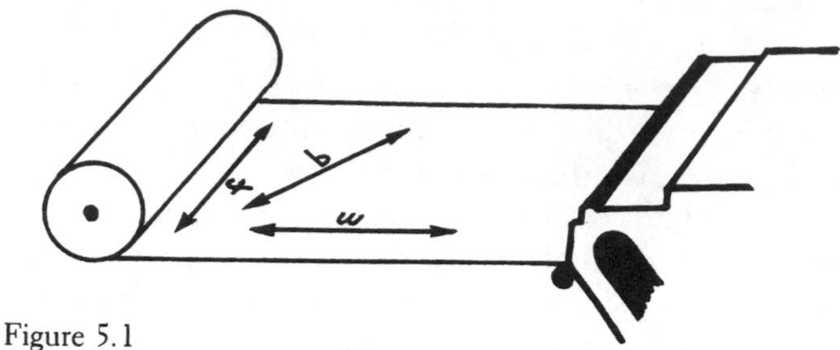

Figure 5.1
Warp (w), fill (f), and (bias) orientations in a roll of fabric coming off a loom.

each at least 10,000 meters long, is arranged to unwind from large spools down the long axis of the loom—a real rigger's nightmare! In the actual weaving process, alternate warp yarns are first lifted, then lowered, while a shuttle carrying the FILL YARN is fired back and forth between them at blinding speed. Figure 5.1 diagrams the orientation of the two threadlines in a length of cloth as it comes off a loom. The BIAS, which is also diagramed, is a term for the diagonal axis of a fabric.

The warp and fill elements of woven materials follow zigzag rather than straight paths. The extent to which a threadline zigzags is called its CRIMP (Figure 5.2). When a piece of woven material is pulled along one of its threadlines, the amount it elongates is determined, not only by thread stretch but also by how much the crimp in those threads straightens out. The more crimp a warp or fill has to start with, the more elastic the fabric will be in that direction.

Looms can be adjusted to put more tension on the warp than the fill, and in some cases, vice versa. It is sometimes also feasible to use larger yarns for one of the threadlines to generate what is called an UNBALANCED WEAVE (Figure 5.2 bottom). When one threadline is tensioned more than the other, the former yarns tend to crimp less while the latter ones are forced to bend more sharply around them.

When large yarns are crossed with smaller ones, the large ones, being stiffer, tend to remain straighter, while the small ones crimp extensively.

Judicious selection of yarn sizes and weaving tensions can produce sailcloths appropriate for different applications. Fabrics for lower aspect sails, including most genoas, are built from balanced or moderately unbalanced weaves (5.3a). Sailcloths for high aspect crosscut mainsails and blade jibs, which must sustain enormous leech loadings, are built from highly unbalanced cloths—large, nearly crimp-free fill yarns crossing a smaller, extensively crimped warp (Figure 5.3b). All else being equal, a more balanced weave will be more resistant to bias stretch which, as we will

Figure 5.2
Crimp in a weave is up and down deflections of the yarns as they bypass one another. In a balanced weave (top) crimp is equal in the warp and the fill. However, in an unbalanced weave (bottom), the smaller yarns crimp substantially more than the larger ones that cross with them.

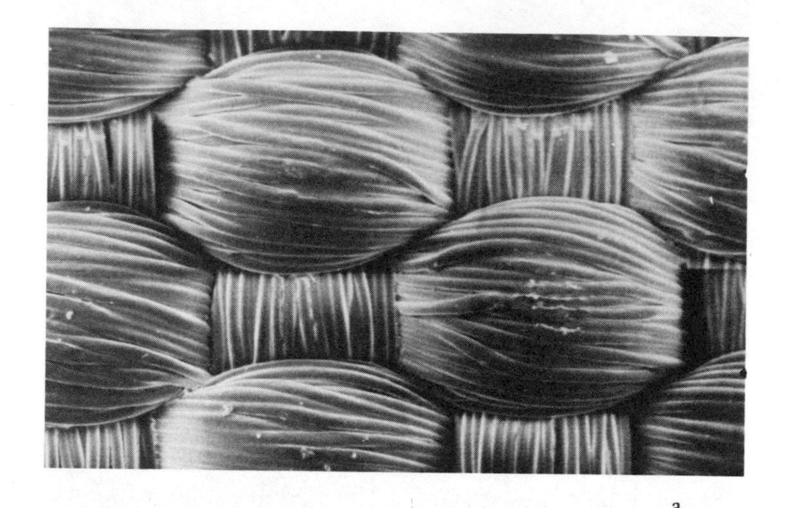

a

b

Figure 5.3

Details of sailcloth weaves are revealed by the scanning electron microscope. Magnification is 77x. The vertically oriented fill yarns of a fairly balanced genoa cloth (photograph a) crimp less than the warp threads, but each contains fewer polyester strands. In contrast, the fill yarns of an unbalanced mainsail cloth (photograph b) are not only larger in diameter, but have less crimp as well. Both fabrics shown weigh about 7½ ounces per sailmakers' yard.

soon see, is the biggest bugaboo faced by sailcloth manufacturers.

In most cases, heavier sailcloths weigh more per yard than lighter ones primarily because they are woven from larger yarns, although weave density and finish are also weight-determining factors.

Lightweight sailcloths tend to be unbalanced in favor of the warp because there is a lower limit to the size of a six-mile-long warp than can withstand the stresses of weaving without breaking too often. History buffs might be amused to learn that vertical panel construction, a sailmaking technique favored in the nineteenth century to take advantage of the warp-favored cotton fabrics of the day, has recently been reintroduced to better utilize the unavoidable unbalance of lightweight polyester weaves.

Sailcloth emerges from weaving mills as GREIGE GOODS (pronounced gray goods) which are shipped to other plants for finishing. Greige goods bear little resemblance to finished sailcloth—they are soft, ragged-edged, and dirty. The finishing process determines to a great extent the properties and quality of a sailcloth and, ultimately, of the sails that will be made from it. To appreciate the significance of the finishing procedures, which will be described in the next chapter, it is necessary to look a bit further at the criteria that define a good sailcloth.

WHAT MAKES GOOD CLOTH GOOD?

The most important properties of a sailcloth are: warp and fill stretch, bias stretch, yield, actual weight, tear resistance, hand, and in some cases, sun resistance, and color. Let's look at these one at a time.

For normal crosscut applications, WARP STRETCH is far less important than FILL STRETCH, because stress lines run-

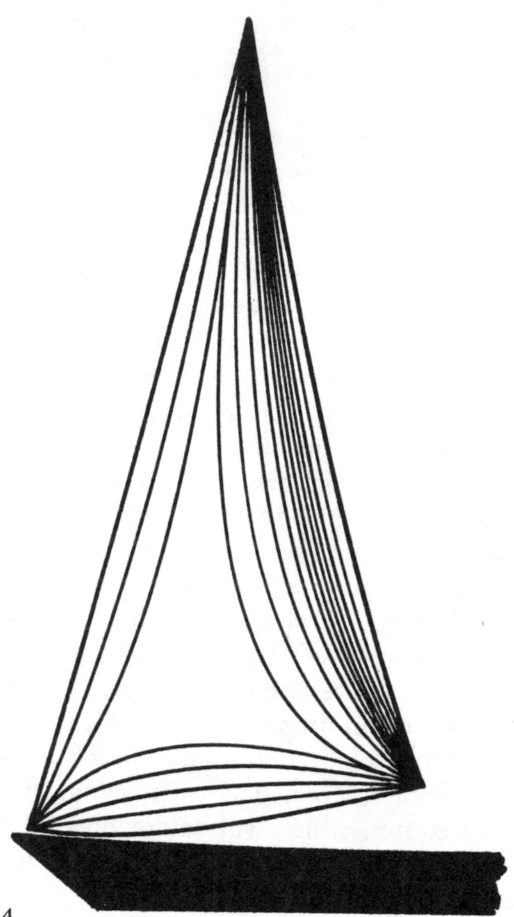

Figure 5.4
A typical pattern of stress distribution in a flying headsail. Where the stress lines are closest together, the load on the sailcloth is greatest. Peak stresses in the sail occur at the head and clew patches. The highest loading in the body of the sail is found a short distance in from the leech.

ning approximately parallel to the leech represent by far the highest loads sustained by the cloth anywhere in the body of a sail (Figure 5.4). For vertical panel sails, of course, the opposite is true.

If the fill yarns of a crosscut headsail (or the warp of a vertical cut sail) stretch excessively, the leech will become loose and fluttery. The excessive leech line required to quiet the stretchy leech will induce a serious hook to windward. If the leech of a mainsail stretches excessively, the batten section will tend to fall off to leeward. Increasing leech tension by tightening the mainsheet will not correct this problem.

BIAS STRETCH in virtually all woven materials is several times greater than threadline stretch for a given load. The bias of an ordinary garment fabric can easily be ten times more elastic than the warp and the fill. The weaves and finishing techniques employed in sailcloth manufacture are, to a large extent, aimed at reducing bias stretch, generally two and a half to four times the favored threadline stretch for a given load. Since even good sailcloth stretches mostly on the bias, it is bias stretch that is primarily to blame when a sail grows deeper in an increasing wind.

Although seldom encountered except in certain types of Mylar® laminate sails, *too little* bias stretch (relative to warp and fill stretch) can also be a problem. Deliberately increasing bias loading near the leading edge of a sail will draw the draft forward—an important sail trimming technique. However, adjusting luff tension is only effective if the bias of the sail is significantly more elastic than the threadlines.

When the material in the luff of a sail is tensioned, it elongates slightly in a direction parallel to the luff, but shortens at right angles to it, as the "squareness" of the weave becomes distorted into an oblique pattern. As a result, the position of maximum depth in the sail is pulled forward, and the entry angle increases (Figure 5.5). An ideal cloth for most applications generally stretches about two and a half times more on bias than on its stronger threadline, but has very low stretch in absolute terms.

Figure 5.5
By tensioning the luff of a sail using the halyard or a Cunningham tackle (right-hand sketch), the position of maximum depth is shifted forward. This change occurs because the weave in the luff area is stretched on the bias as illustrated in the enlarged diagrams.

A sailcloth is said to YIELD when it is stretched to the point that permanent deformation results. Obviously, it is highly desirable to avoid using a sail in a situation where it will yield, but if an inappropriate cloth was selected, this may be impossible.

The ACTUAL WEIGHT of a sailcloth is important because, to a large extent, cloth weight determines the ease with which a sail will fill and hence the minimum wind velocity it requires to become effective. Discussing the weight of sailcloth can be confusing because there are several standards in effect. In North America weights are given in ounces per sailmakers' yard which for some strange reason is a rectangle 28½ by 36 inches!

The importance of TEAR RESISTANCE in a sailcloth needs no explanation. However, for reasons that will become apparent in the next chapter, achieving adequate tear resistance often involves compromising other cloth qualities such as stretch resistance and weight.

The HAND of a sailcloth refers to its softness and flexibility—basically how pleasant, or unpleasant, it is to touch and handle. Again, achieving a satisfactory hand will often compromise certain other desired features in a sailcloth.

Ultraviolet light from sunshine degrades all sailcloths. Kevlar® and nylon are particularly vulnerable. In tropical climates ultraviolet coatings are crucially important if a sailcloth is to have reasonable longevity.

Colored sails may seem to be primarily an aesthetic consideration, but the difficult process of dyeing polyester generally interferes substantially with subsequent finishing steps and compromises the cloth in other respects. Nylon, on the other hand, dyes easily with no unpleasant side effects.

6 Sailcloth Finishing and Testing

THE most important physical properties of sailcloth—warp, fill and bias stretch, yield, actual weight, tear resistance, hand, sun resistance and color—are largely determined by the way it is finished rather than the way it is woven. Sailcloth finishing operations are normally performed, not at the weaving mills that produce the greige goods, but at separate finishing plants. In North America, most sailcloth is woven in the southeastern United States, while most finishing plants are in New England, close to the head offices of the sailcloth manufacturers.

The principal techniques employed in sailcloth finishing are heat setting, dyeing (in the case of colored fabrics), resin impregnation, resin coating, calendaring, and plying (lamination). Although there are other steps, too, ranging from scouring the greige goods to trimming, packaging, and shipping the finished sailcloth, I will concentrate on those that have a direct effect upon sailcloth performance.

HEAT SETTING

Although polyester greige goods intended for sailcloth are generally woven as tightly as possible, there are practical limits to tensions that yarns can sustain during weaving. Yarn breakages cause expensive interruptions in loom operation. Fortunately, polyester shrinks about 15 percent when heated close to its melting point. Sailcloth finishers take advantage of this to tighten their weaves. Since heat setting causes the threads to interlock more tightly with each other, its primary effect is to improve resistance to bias stretch. Threadline stretch resistance improves, at best, only slightly, because in the process of increasing weave density, heat shrinking also increases crimp.

If the cloth is gripped tightly by rows of jaws at opposite sides of the panel while being run through the shrinking oven, the fill will remain relatively straight, while the crimp in the warp increases dramatically. This technique can be used to improve bias characteristics while, at the same time, making a cloth more unbalanced.

DYEING

Most polyester sailcloths are not dyed, and for good reason. Polyester molecules have few binding sites where dye molecules can adhere; to color it satisfactorily is a difficult process involving high temperatures and harsh chemicals. If goods are yarn dyed (dyed before weaving) it is impossible to heat set the weave properly, because the dyeing process has already shrunk the yarns. Piece dyeing is only slightly more satisfactory, because the chemicals employed tend to interfere with subsequent resinating procedures. The most satisfactory applications for colored sailcloths are those from which only modest fabric performance is expected.

In the case of nylon spinnaker cloths, dyeing is an altogether different story. Nylon molecules have plenty of good dye-binding sites, so excellent results can be obtained with only minimal harm to the mechanical properties of the finished fabric.

a

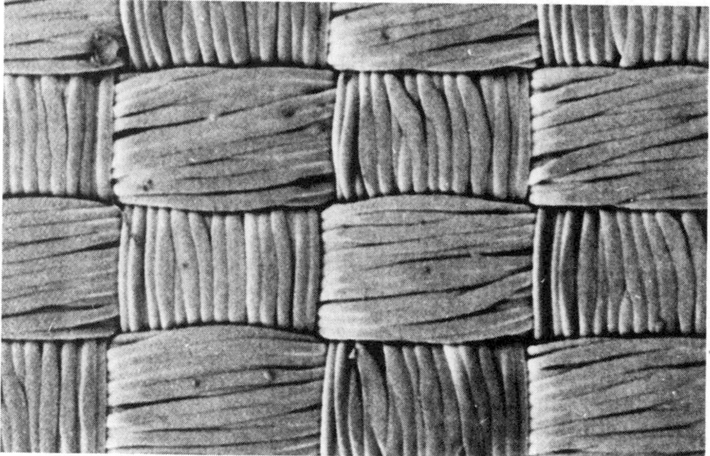

b

Figure 6.1

Scanning electron microscope views of a 3.8-ounce weave finished in different ways. Magnification is 64x. Photograph a shows a soft, lightly resin impregnated cloth. The fabric in photograph b was heavily impregnated with melamine resin and flattened substantially in the calendaring

c

d

process. New resin coated cloth is shown in photograph c, while photograph d reveals some effects of wear (about four times the industries' standard flutter test) upon the urethane resin coating of the same material.

RESIN IMPREGNATION

Plastic resins are commonly employed to bind or cement together the yarns of a weave and the strands that make up the yarns. Naturally, this stabilizes a sailcloth and makes it more resistant to stretch, both along the threadlines and on the bias. The most common resinating technique involves immersing cloth in a solution of catalyzed melamine resin—a plastic not very different from the polyesters used to make polyester yarns or, for that matter, fiberglass boats. Using different varieties and concentrations of melamine in the solution, a manufacturer can produce a range of sailcloths, all based on a single weave, that vary radically in terms of hand (softness) and stability or stretch resistance (Figure 6.1 a & b). Ordinarily, resin impregnated fabrics are heat set following immersion in the resin bath to allow the heat treatment to "kick off" or accelerate the polymerization of the melamine in addition to shrinking the weave.

RESIN COATING

The most stable non-laminated sailcloths are those made by coating one side of the weave with a resin film (Figure 6.1c). This operation is performed by running the cloth through a trough of viscous, catalyzed urethane resin. A steel blade bearing against the surface of the cloth as it emerges from the trough scrapes off excess resin. The urethane coating polymerizes to form a tough, although fairly flexible film on the surface of the weave. In contrast to resin impregnation, which, for the most part, cements together the individual strands that make up the yarns and stiffens the yarns themselves, resin coating locks together the weave as a whole. The resulting material has a stiff, crisp hand. Sails made from these so-called yarn-tempered materials (technically a Howe and Bainbridge trade name® although the process is now used by all sailcloth manufacturers) should be carefully rolled, never just stuffed into bags. Even if not abused, these urethane coatings gradually break down as the sail is used (Figure 6.1d). On the other hand, sails made from resin coated fabrics are extremely stable for their weights.

CALENDARING

Many sailcloths are subjected to a treatment called calendaring which involves running the fabric between hot steel rollers which are pressed together with forces measured in tons per linear inch. The calendaring process crushes the weave, stabilizing the cloth and smoothing its surface. The resin impregnated cloth sample shown in Figure 6.1b clearly shows the effects of calendaring upon the surface of the weave.

MYLAR® LAMINATION

Although Mylar® sailcloth is usually regarded as something more than just ordinary cloth that has been finished a bit differently, it is, in fact, logical to consider the application of a Mylar® film to a woven substrate as simply another finishing procedure. Modern Mylar® laminates are achieved by bonding, using catalyzed polyester resin adhesives and roller pressure. The result is not dissimilar to that produced by resin coating—a woven substrate covered with a homogeneous plastic film (Figure 6.2).

Of course there are important differences. Since Mylar® (polyester) films are tougher and less brittle than the urethane layers on coated sailcloth, it is practical to design Mylar® laminate sailcloths with the film component bear-

Figure 6.2
A laminated sailcloth sample with a section of the Mylar® film peeled back to reveal the polyester taffeta substrate. The relatively small area of adhesive contact created a material with only modest resistance to delamination in this case. Magnification is 22x.

ing a far greater proportion of the total load. In fact, the first Mylar® laminate materials depended entirely upon the Mylar® film to sustain sailing loads. The light, stretchy nylon substrates used initially served only to supplement the tear resistance of the otherwise exceedingly rip prone Mylar®.

Before long, sailcloth manufacturers realized that there was no reason to let the substrate tag along without doing any real work. As mentioned earlier, polyester yarns are actually more stretch resistant, pound for pound, than polyester films because the long polymer molecules in a yarn become aligned into parallel arrays during extrusion while those in a film remain randomly oriented. Since the highest loads in a sail run parallel to the leech, it makes sense to use the yarns of the substrate to reinforce the Mylar® film along the axis of highest loading.

SOPHISTICATED SUBSTRATES

Although yarns themselves are highly stretch resistant, crimp introduced during the weaving process invariably makes a given threadline substantially more elastic. In conventional sailcloths, the very tightly interlocking weaves needed to control bias stretch have too much crimp to provide maximal resistance to threadline stretch. However, in a Mylar® laminate, the Mylar® film does an excellent job of controlling bias stretch, so a loosely constructed, low crimp polyester taffeta makes a highly satisfactory substrate.

Like other light weaves, substrate taffetas (Figure 6.3a) tend to be warp favored—hence most commercial Mylar® laminates were, until recently, best suited to vertical panel construction. However, this situation is changing. Two other types of substrates for Mylar® lamination are becoming increasingly popular: scrims and knits. Scrims are netlike woven materials with large, widely spaced yarns. Since the yarns are far apart, there is virtually no crimp to straighten under load.

Knits (Figure 6.3b) are also comprised of large, widely spaced yarns, but the two threadlines don't interlock at all. A third set of fine yarns running in a diagonal direction loops around the major yarns to hold them together prior to lamination. Both knits and scrims can be constructed to favor either the warp or, more commonly, the fill depending upon application intended.

The strongest sailcloths for their weights are laminates of Mylar® film and a substrate employing Kevlar® yarns oriented with the high load axis. Since any crimp in the Kevlar® nullifies the potential advantage of its very high strength-to-weight ratio, scrim or knit constructions are usually used. Although exceedingly strong, Kevlar® is inelastic and can be deformed only slightly before it breaks.

a

Figure 6.3
Different styles of substrates for Mylar® laminates. Photograph a shows a taffeta magnified 53x. The low resistance to bias stretch of the loose, low crimp weave is evidenced by the fact that in this case, the "squareness" of the substrate weave was distorted when it was bonded to the Mylar® film. Photograph b shows a knit substrate magnified 15x. Large, ribbon-like fill yarns are overlaid with much smaller warp yarns. The even smaller diagonal yarns hold the warp and fill in position prior to lamination.

b

Folding or crumpling a sail involves bending some yarns to very small radii, producing tremendous localized strains within the strands of these yarns. Thus Kevlar® reinforced sails are vulnerable to failure if handled roughly, and often have short lives. Sailcloth containing Kevlar® is currently three to four times more expensive than conventional sailcloths or Mylar® laminates intended for the same application. The recent, controversial ban on sails containing Kevlar® by the International Ocean Racing Council was a response to these drawbacks.

CLOTH TESTING

Sailcloth manufacturers constantly test their products and, in most cases, routinely furnish copies of the results to their sailmaking customers. In addition, many sailmakers, particularly large firms, use their own testing equipment to verify the data furnished by manufacturers.

The basic procedure used to evaluate sailcloth is a STRESS/STRAIN TEST—subjecting a sample to a progressively increasing load (stress) and measuring how much it deforms (strain). Samples for stress/strain tests are cut from cloth panels in three standard orientations (to evaluate each of the threadlines and the bias). Samples can be pretreated to imitate the effects of service. Additional tests are used to evaluate the ability of fabrics to resist tearing, air leakage, and for plyed materials, delamination.

INTERPRETING CLOTH TEST DATA

Most sailcloth test samples are strips of material 16 inches long and 2 inches wide—the size of test samples used in the Instron® testing machines which are standard equipment in many industrial and scientific laboratories. Instron® testers,

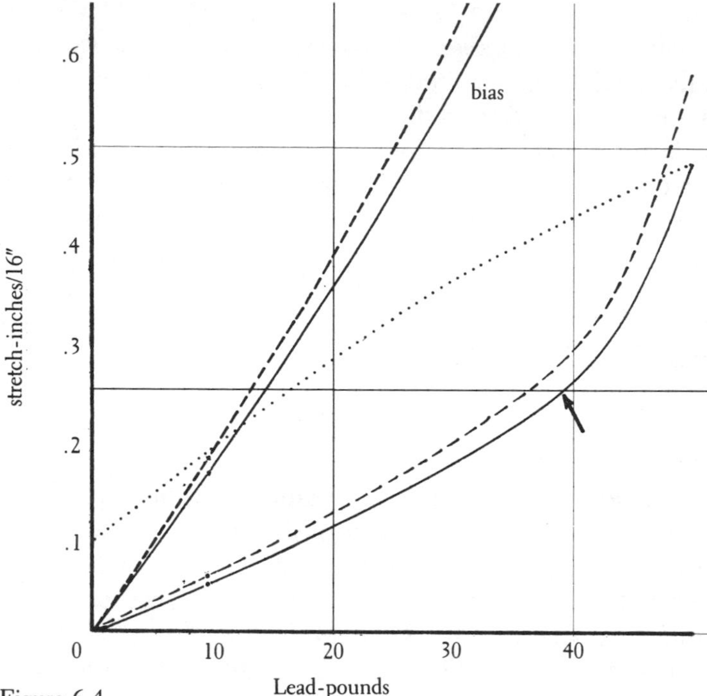

Figure 6.4

A facsimile of a typical cloth test graph. Solid lines represent data from virgin samples (so-called lab samples). Dashed lines are data from fluttered samples. Ten-pound figures for the cloth in this example are 5 to 16 lab, 6 to 17½ after flutter. The fill yields at a little over forty pounds as shown by the arrow. Dotted line shows how fill sample would "relax" after being loaded to fifty pounds. Note the permanent elongation even after the stress has returned to zero.

as well as more specialized, custom-made cloth testing machines, grasp the test sample in a pair of jaws and pull on it. The testing machine is programed to increase the tensile force on the sample at a steady rate to a preset maximum value; then steadily reduce the load back to zero. While the testing machine is stressing the cloth sample, it automatically measures the strain (elongation) and draws a graph of stress against strain. Sailcloth samples are rarely tested to failure, because most will have deformed to the point of uselessness long before they actually break.

A conventional sailcloth graph plots stress on the X-axis against elongation (of a standard 16-inch sample) on the Y-axis in hundredths of inches (Figure 6.4). It is common practice to use just two numbers from the graphs to provide a brief description of a fabric's stretch characteristics. Ten-pound figures of 6 to 22 mean that a standard-sized sample of a particular sailcloth stretches 6 one-hundredths of an inch on the fill and 22 one-hundredths of an inch on the bias when subjected to a ten-pound load. Ten-pound figures are useful mainly for comparing different cloths because the real loads sustained by the fabric of most sails in brisk winds are much higher. It's generally a good idea to examine and compare fifty-pound figures as well, and in some cases even one hundred-pound or one hundred fifty-pound stretch values.

Of particular interest are the YIELD POINTS of a sailcloth which generally show up on test graphs as a fairly abrupt increase in the rate of stretch under steadily increasing load. Once loaded beyond its yield point in a particular direction, a fabric stretches comparatively rapidly and, in most cases, permanently. The amount of permanent elongation can be measured when the tension on the sample in a testing machine is eased back to zero and the final length of the sample compared to its original length. Unless a sailcloth has a very gradual or "soft" yield, it is crucial to avoid using it in applications where its yield value will be exceeded.

To evaluate the effects of use upon the stretch resistance of a sailcloth, the most common procedure is called a flutter test. The original test, attributed to Lowell North, consisted of attaching strips of cloth to an automobile antenna and driving at 35 mph for thirty minutes. Today, this treatment

a

Figure 6.5

Shifting yarns spread the load over a wide area in a soft, loosely woven garment fabric, making it highly resistant to tearing (photograph a). In contrast, the thread yarns of a resin coated sailcloth can move only slightly and tend to break one at a time (photograph b). Magnification 36x.

b

is usually imitated indoors with an electric fan. Following flutter, fabric stretch is measured in a cloth testing machine to see how much the material has deteriorated. Our sample that gave ten-pound figures of 6 to 22 fresh off the roll, might test 7 to 24 after flutter.

It takes a little while, but after examining and comparing a few sailcloth test graphs (if possible with the help of a sailmaker) you can really begin to appreciate differences between sailcloths and to understand how particular fabrics are matched to particular applications.

TESTING TEAR RESISTANCE

Loosely woven materials such as garment fabrics are comparatively difficult to puncture or tear because individual yarns tend to slide away from concentrated loads, shifting neighboring yarns and forcing them to share the load in the process (Figure 6.5a). Sailcloths on the other hand, are very tightly woven, and in many cases treated with resins, to minimize bias stretch. Consequently, the movement of the individual yarns within a sailcloth is curtailed and they are more prone to fracture one after another like a chain of falling dominoes (Figure 6.5b). Mylar® films lacking any woven substrate are the worst of all. In general, the more stable a sailcloth is for its weight, the more easily it will tear. One must compromise.

Tear resistance is measured essentially by nailing a sample of sailcloth to a board and measuring the force needed to propagate a tear by using a spring scale. It's even easier to get a rough-and-ready idea of tear resistance by judging how much force is needed to extend a tear that was started with a scissors nick at the edge of a small sample. Differences are often dramatic.

OTHER TESTS

In the days of cotton sailcloth, the leakage of air through sails from the high pressure side to the low pressure side degraded racing performance enough so that it was sometimes advantageous to wet the sails in order to seal them better. The weaving and finishing techniques used on modern sailcloths in most cases makes them virtually airtight, at least when new. To test POROSITY, cloth samples are used to block off the end of a pressure chamber, and the rate of leakage measured.

PEEL TESTS, used to evaluate the strength of the bond between a Mylar® film and its substrate, are much like tear tests. A scale is used to measure the force required to strip the Mylar off a sailcloth sample.

Two additional classes of tests used to assess the properties of sailcloths are ULTRAVIOLET DEGRADATION TESTS to determine resistance to sunlight, and WASH TESTS to determine how well particular finishes resist water damage. Generally these procedures are combined with stress/strain testing to evaluate the effects of weathering on the fabric's mechanical performance.

7 Commercial Sail Manufacture

THE topics discussed so far in this book—sail function, flying shapes, sail design, and fabric properties—have paved the way for a look at the snip and stitch side of sailmaking. This chapter focuses attention on how sails are cut, assembled, and finished in most production lofts.

Six fundamental steps are involved in building a sail. First, during LAYOUT, the shapes of the edges of the constituent panels are drawn. The second step, CUTTING, as the name suggests, basically means trimming away excess cloth outside some of the panel perimeters. SEAMING, the third step, is sewing and/or gluing the panels together in their proper positions with respect to each other. The following stage, often called SECOND LAYOUT, involves fairing, and in some cases, cutting the luff, leech, and foot curves. FINISHING, the fifth step in sail manufacture, includes attaching fabric reinforcements in highly stressed regions, and sewing tapes and/or ropes to the luff, leech, and foot. HANDWORK, the end of the sailmaking process, involves attaching fittings such as rings, hanks, and slides. Let's look at each step in more detail.

Figure 7.1
A computer controlled X-Y plotter marks the edges of sail panels at North Sails, San Francisco. The carriage bearing the marking pen can simultaneously and automatically move along the table and across it. The sailcloth strip is held in position on the steel tabletop with magnetic clips.

LAYOUT

Full-scale layout on the loft floor is a traditional technique still used by many sailmakers today. The intended sail is outlined using string, pencil, or self-adhesive tape. Allowances must be made for roach curves, convex luffs, and foot round. For maximum cloth economy, allowances should also be made for hollow luffs and leeches. Next, strips of cloth (PANELS) are unrolled over the outline and cut off, leaving a small excess for trimming. Selvage guide lines, normally drawn 12mm or 18mm (½″ or ¾″) from the edges of the sailcloth by the cloth manufacturer, serve as an aid in overlapping the panels for a uniform seam allowance. Once all the panels are lying in position on the floor, reference marks are penciled across the edges of adjacent panels to permit reassembly in the same relative positions during the seaming step.

Today, it is increasingly common to lay out the panels of

a sail one at a time on a CUTTING TABLE. Dimensional data for individual panel cutting is furnished, either from a precise scale drawing or a computer generated analog of a scale drawing. Table layout requires less space than floor layout, which reduces overhead costs in some cases. It is generally preferred by sailmaking personnel because it is more comfortable to work standing than kneeling. When table layout is used, broadseaming is generally marked and cut at the same time that the panels themselves are trimmed to size. The most sophisticated layout systems are computer controlled X-Y plotters which automatically draw or cut the outlines of all the panels of a sail on a continuous length of sailcloth stretched out on a long table (Figure 7.1).

BROADSEAMING

As was discussed in Chapters 1 and 4, some of the panels of most sails are tapered rather than uniform in width, a feature that contributes to the camber of the sail in use. A tapered panel is created from cloth of uniform width by building tapered seams. These are commonly called BROADSEAMS because they are wider near the luff or leech and narrower at the center of the sail (Figure 7.2). Where so much broadseaming is used that the amount of overlap might be considered unsightly, the excess can be trimmed away. The effect upon sail shape remains the same.

When the edges of panels are trimmed for broadseaming or in any other situation where an unhemmed edge will be exposed to wear, it is considered good sailmaking practice to HEAT SEAL the edge. This operation is performed by cutting the fabric with an electric hot-knife rather than with scissors. Heavily resinated fabrics and Mylar® laminates are sufficiently resistant to unraveling so that this precaution can be safely omitted.

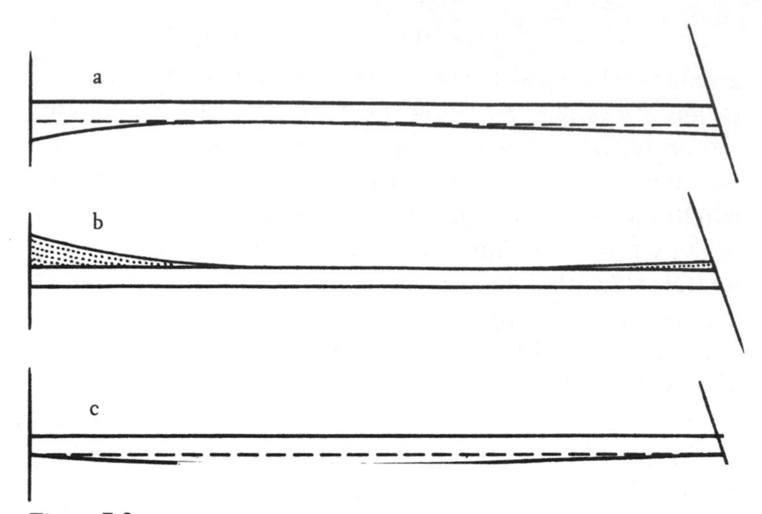

Figure 7.2
Standard broadseam (top), trimmed broadseam (middle), and negative broadseam (bottom). Dashed line indicates position of selvage mark provided, in most cases, by the sailcloth manufacturer. The shaded areas in the middle sketch represent fabric that was trimmed away.

Occasionally, negative broadseams—those which overlap to a greater extent in the middle of a sail than at the luff or leech—are introduced to remove excessive fullness stemming from fabric stretch (Figure 7.2 bottom). Negative broadseams are mainly used on certain heavy weather headsails.

After the edges of the individual panels are marked and trimmed it is, of course, necessary to attach them together permanently. In almost all cases, the seams of sails are fastened primarily if not exclusively with stitching. Sewing machines used for seaming sails are light- to moderate-duty industrial models, preferably equipped with extra long arms so that even large sails can be rolled up and passed through easily. Seaming machines are often equipped with power-driven pullers or rollers to help feed the work evenly.

Sails are usually seamed with polyester thread using a

zigzag stitch for better tear resistance (Figure 7.3 top). In general, sails lighter than six ounces are seamed with two rows of stitching. Heavier sails get three rows. Dinghy sails are often seamed using single passes on a three-step sewing machine which produces a zigzag pattern in a row of straight stitches (Figure 7.3 bottom). Straight, even rows of stitching are desirable for cosmetic reasons, but the strength of a seam is rarely compromised by irregularities unless a row of stitching wanders outside the area where the two adjoining panels overlap. On the whole, it is more important that the stitch tension be uniform and that the tension along the edges of the two panels being joined is equal.

During the seaming operation, it is crucial that the edge of one panel remains perfectly aligned with the selvage line on the adjacent panel. Errors here create conspicuous irregularities in the curvature of the flying sail. To make seam alignment easier, some sailmakers tape the seams together in advance, usually using double-sided tape (adhesive on

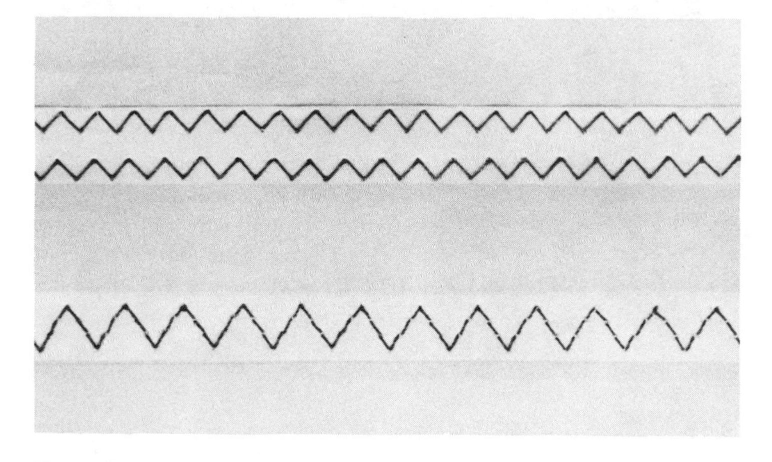

Figure 7.3
Standard half-inch seam assembled with two rows of zigzag stitching (top), or a single pass with a two-step sewing machine (bottom).

Figure 7.4
The luff of a sail is fanned by positioning a fold of cloth a short distance behind the luff itself. This technique, in effect, excludes most of the influence of broadseaming from the immediate luff area so that the shape of a luff curve can be accurately judged.

both faces). Others fit devices to their seaming machines that maintain a constant overlap as the operator pushes the panels through.

With laminated sail materials now an accepted part of modern sailmaking, experiments are underway to develop quick, strong bonded seams to replace stitched ones. However, it is considerably more difficult to reliably glue narrow seams on a cutting table or sail loft floor, than wide rolls of material in a laminating plant. Satisfactory techniques will, no doubt, be developed in time.

SECOND LAYOUT

Once a sail is seamed, a sailmaker using conventional techniques unrolls the sail on the loft floor over the original layout lines. At this point, the final positions of head, tack, and clew are marked on the cloth; positions marked originally will have shifted somewhat as a result of broadseaming.

The next step, a critical one, is to draw in the luff curve. Since no sail with any appreciable amount of broadseaming will lie flat on the floor once it is assembled, a sailmaker uses a technique called FANNING to persuade the edge of the sail he or she is currently working on to lie flat. To fan a luff, for example, the sailmaker "throws" a fold into the sail that runs parallel to, and a foot or so inside, the luff itself (Figure 7.4). Once satisfied that the cloth near the luff itself is lying fairly and smoothly, the sailmaker draws in the luff curve desired. Several methods can be used to produce a fair curve. The most common involves bending a long wooden or fiberglass lofting batten around several pins (sailmakers' awls) thrust into the floor. The luff curve is then marked, the sail unfanned and, if the shape of the curve still appears satisfactory, the luff is cut. Getting consistently good luff curves using traditional methods requires a good eye and lots of experience.

A similar approach is used to fair leech and leech curves, but since these have less impact on the ultimate flying shape of the sail, they are less critical.

With developments in computerized sail design, it has become feasible to automatically predict the effects of broadseaming upon the positions of a small number of key points that describe a desired luff curve. Modern design programs make it practical to mark out the luff curve and, in some cases, the leech and foot curves, too, when the individual panels are first laid out. Following seaming, it is necessary only to "connect the dots" and perhaps confirm that the curve looks OK before trimming the edges of the sail.

In many cases, reef reinforcements and head, tack, and clew patches are sized and positioned while the sail is on the floor for second layout. Again, however, the trend is toward performing more of these operations, which in a sense are really sail design operations, during the initial design stage. Today, in many lofts, the patches themselves are attached before the sail is completely seamed, while the parts of the sail are smaller and easier to handle.

FINISHING

The attachment of sewn reinforcements, edge tapes, ropes, and tablings (hems) are ordinarily considered finishing operations, whether performed following second layout, or earlier in the sailmaking process. Head, clew, tack, and reef REINFORCING PATCHES are normally constructed from multiple layers of sailcloth cut to different sizes (Figure 7.5). The overall aim is to produce a reinforced area, the strength of which varies in proportion to changes in local

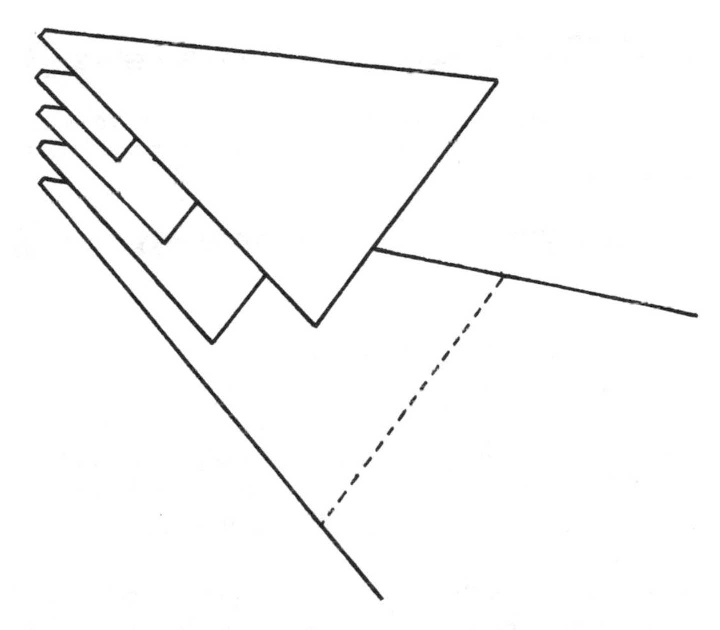

Figure 7.5
Exploded view of a typical triangular head reinforcement. For cosmetic reasons, the large cover patch is ordinarily made of the same sailcloth as the body of the sail.

fabric loading. Since head and clew loads are usually much higher than tack loads, tack patches can be considerably smaller and lighter. Triangular patch profiles are most common, although a look at stress distribution patterns (see Figure 5.4), particularly near the clew of a sail, suggests that other shapes can be expected to perform more satisfactorily. In fact, sailmakers frequently experiment with the design and construction of their patches in an effort to reduce localized distortion in their sails, or to make them less expensive to manufacture.

The luff leech and foot of all sails are finished in one of two basic ways. Edges which are not supported by spars or headstays (i.e. all leeches and the feet of most headsails) are

Figure 7.6

Diagrammatic cross sections of various edge-finishing details: double-fold tabling (a), taped edge (b), internal boltrope (c), and prefabricated tape for a slotted headfoil (d).

tabled or taped. A TABLING is made by folding the sailcloth over one or more times to create a hem which is then sewn down (Figure 7.6a). TAPING is performed by sewing a folded strip of sailcloth with heat-sealed edges over the raw edge of the sail (Figure 7.6b). If a leech line or foot line is desired for trim adjustment, it is slipped under the tabling or tape at this time.

Luffs, as well as the feet of most mainsails, are treated somewhat differently, because they must be attached to spars or wires during use. These edges are usually fitted with an INTERNAL BOLTROPE which either slides directly into a groove in a mast, boom, or headstay foil or serves as reinforcement to keep the sail from distorting excessively when spaced hanks or slides are used to fasten sail to rigging. The luff or foot is taped with a MESSENGER LINE (much like a leechline) inside. The messenger line is then used to pull through a length of polyester or nylon rope which is then sewn down at each end (Figure 7.6c). Getting the proper amount of pre-tension on the luff tape and the rope inside it is critically important if the sail is to fly and behave well. Many sailmakers use spring scales and consult data tables at this stage of construction.

Headsails built for grooved headstay foils are often finished with PREFABRICATED LUFF TAPES. These tapes usually contain stiff, hard, braided line that is difficult to compress and hence resistant to popping out of the groove.

Some types have two or more ropes behind one another to accommodate feeding mechanisms or further stiffen the tape (Figure 7.6d). Obviously the correct size and type of tape must be selected for the gear to be used.

EXTERNAL, SEWN-ON ROPES, once commonly used on the luff, the foot, and even the leech of a sail, are seldom seen anymore. Likewise, stainless steel or galvanized LUFF WIRES, once commonly employed inside the luff tapes of headsails, are rarely used today because they make it impossible to adjust fore-and-aft draft location by altering tension on the sailcloth near the luff. Their modern application is for staysails and free-luff drifters. In these cases, the internal luff wire assumes the role of a headstay and is anchored to the sail only at the head. The luff tape and so-called FLOATING TACK are free to slide over the wire, permitting luff tension adjustments.

Most mainsails, and some heavy weather headsails, employ battens to help support their leech areas. BATTEN POCKETS are constructed and fitted as part of sail finishing. Good ones generally employ an elastic loop at the forward (inner) end to force the batten back against the aft end of the pocket, and are heavily reinforced and sewn to resist chafe.

HANDWORK

A wide variety of hardware items and techniques are used to complete different types of sails (Figure 7.7). Headsail luffs are often attached to headstays with HANKS made of bronze, plastic, or occasionally stainless steel. Similarly, plastic or metal SLIDES and SLUGS are used to fasten mainsails to the tracks and grooves on spars. Hanks, slides, and slugs are SEIZED (lashed), shackled, or fastened with loops of nylon webbing through small CRINGLES (grommets) set a short distance behind the luff of the sail.

Figure 7.7
Assorted sail hardware. Top row from right to left: internal slide, external slide, nylon slug. Middle row: D-ring, headboard, aluminum head/clew slug. Bottom row: spur grommets, pressed-in ring, plastic hank, and bronze hank.

At one time, these grommets as well as the larger rings at the corners of sails were HANDWORKED. Supporting metal rings were hand stitched to the edges of a hole made in a sail and a thin metal liner pressed into place to protect the stitching from chafe. Today, most sailmakers use SPUR GROMMETS for small cringles and PRESSED-IN RINGS for large ones, although a few traditionalist lofts continue to use handworked rings.

The top and bottom halves of a spur grommet are inserted through a punched hole in the sail and crimped together by a mallet blow on a pair of interlocking dies. A similar approach is used to insert pressed-in rings at corners of sails. In this case a hydraulic press is required to force the dies together hard enough to flair the ends of the fairly thick stainless steel liner that ultimately holds together a set of tooth-studded washers on each face of the reinforcing patch. Modern pressed-in rings, correctly inserted, are demonstrably stronger than handworked rings of similar size.

The clews of large sails, and the heads and tacks of many furling sails are fitted with D-RINGS rather than pressed-in rings. These rings, bent and welded out of stainless steel rod and shaped like the letter "D," are attached to the corners of sails by loops of NYLON WEBBING (similar to narrow seat belt material) which are sewn to the patches using heavy duty industrial machines.

Numerous other operations are performed on one sort of sail or another: battens are fitted, headboards and clewboards installed, sail numbers and draft-visualization stripes applied, leech line cleats and buttons affixed, and leather chafe patches sewn into place. Many sails are specialized items, and the variety of procedures used to make them is too great to discuss in exhaustive detail. In most sail lofts, each completed sail is inspected, and in many cases, test flown, before it is bagged and delivered.

8 Spinnaker Design and Construction

ALTHOUGH spinnakers are often considered to be entirely different from "ordinary" sails, they affect air flow, deform under load, and respond to trim in the same ways that other sails do. This chapter will emphasize the parallels between modern spinnaker building and the sail-making practices described so far. There are differences, of course, but I expect you will emerge with the impression that spinnakers, although "cats of a different color" (usually in more ways than one), are "cats" nonetheless.

SPINNAKER CLOTH

Since synthetic sailcloths supplanted cottons, beginning in the late 1950s, woven nylon has, almost without exception, been the type of fabric selected for building spinnakers. Pound for pound, nylons are often slightly stronger than polyesters. More important, they are much more elastic. Knowing that substantial stretchiness is considered a serious drawback in working sails, how can it be an advantage for spinnakers? The key difference is the way that spinnakers are flown. Unlike mainsails and headsails, the actual weight of which is predominantly borne by spars and standing rigging, the weight of a flying spinnaker must be largely or, better yet, completely, counterbalanced by the aerodynamic forces acting on the sail itself. Of course, problems arise in light winds. Consequently, minimum cloth weight is a much higher priority for spinnakers than for working sails. A 100-square meter (about 1,100 square foot) "all purpose" spinnaker is ordinarily built from fabric weighing nine-tenths of an ounce per sailmakers' yard. In contrast, cloth for a 60 square meter (650 square foot) light #1 genoa seldom weighs less than four ounces per sailmakers' yard. As a result, spinnakers frequently operate a lot closer to breaking loads than other sails. The elasticity of nylon fabrics often enables spinnakers to survive high shock loads such as those produced when the sail refills suddenly after collapsing in a stiff breeze.

Stretchy spinnaker fabrics may have another advantage. Experimental low-stretch spinnakers made of materials such as light Mylar® laminates have so far been unsuccessful, not only because these sails were too delicate, but because they were excessively tricky to fly. Apparently some give is necessary to make a spinnaker manageable, particularly in light winds and rough water.

Spinnaker cloths are ordinarily woven in a RIP-STOP PATTERN—every fifteenth thread or so in both the warp and the fill is larger than the others (Figure 8.1). Small tears tend to stop when they encounter a large thread, preventing extensive damage in some cases. Most spinnaker cloth has a balanced weave. However, with the increasing popularity of radial construction, high sley spinnaker cloth—material woven to favor the warp—is being manufactured and sold.

Because the weave itself is light and elastic, the mechanical properties of spinnaker fabrics are dramatically affected by resin finishes. So-called half-ounce spinnaker cloth (actual weight about three-fourths of an ounce per sailmakers'

Figure 8.1
A balanced one and a half ounce spinnaker cloth magnified 64x. Note the larger rip-stop yarn oriented vertically to the right of center.

yard) is the lightest material in common use and is most affected by the finish selected. Plastic finishing resins are less flexible than nylon yarns, so a half-ounce spinnaker cloth with a firm resin coating is often more stable than a softer three-quarter ounce spinnaker cloth (weighing over nine-tenths of an ounce per yard), but is much easier to tear, break, or deform permanently as a result of overload.

CONTEMPORARY SPINNAKER DESIGN

Until the early 1970s, virtually all spinnaker panel layouts were variations of a basic HORIZONTAL or CROSS-CUT pattern in which all the panels ran more or less parallel to the foot (Figure 8.2a). In some versions, a vertical center seam or MITER SEAM up the midline of the symmetrical sail

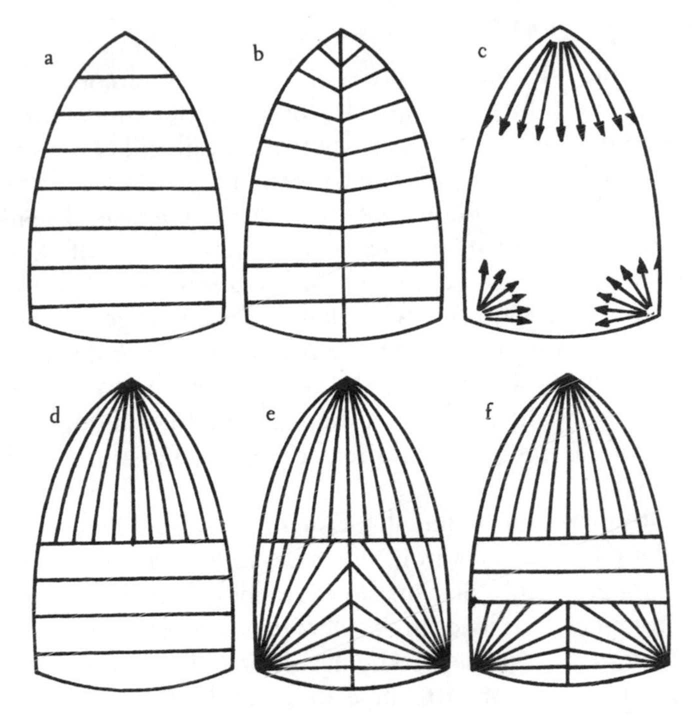

Figure 8.2
Spinnaker design has evolved away from the horizontal and modified horizontal types (a and b), because the principal stresses within the sail radiate from the head and clews (c). Radial head spinnakers (d) were a design breakthrough because they eliminated the most serious distortions caused by cloth stretch. Starcuts (e) and tri-radials (f) are further refinements of the radial concept.

formed a dividing line between panels that angled up toward each leech (Figure 8.2b). These designs all suffered a common shortcoming: the stresses near the head and clews of a spinnaker radiate more or less uniformly from each corner (Figure 8.2c). No matter how a panel of fabric is oriented as it passes across the head or clew of a spinnaker, in some areas the axis of maximum stress will parallel one of the threadlines while in others it will swing onto the bias. As a result, all horizontally cut spinnakers distort non-uniformly as they load up. The most conspicuous deformation is usually near the head where these sails either become V-shaped or W-shaped in cross section.

The development of the RADIAL HEAD spinnaker (Figure 8.2d) pretty much eliminated the most serious of these faults. Radial heads are comprised of a series of fairly narrow pie-shaped panels with slightly convex edges. When these are sewn together, a three-dimensional curved surface is formed. Nowhere is the threadline more than a few degrees out of alignment with the load axis so, although the head of the spinnaker still stretches, it stretches almost uniformly.

Of course, once the shape of the head could be kept under reasonable control, sailors began to carry spinnakers in stronger winds, and on closer reaches. Under these circumstances, bias loads in the clew areas led to unacceptable distortions in sail shape. The next logical development was RADIAL CLEW. At first, these were employed in so-called STARCUT designs—spinnakers on which the radial head and two radial clew all met up with one another at the center of the sails (Figure 8.2e). Subsequently, sailmakers learned that it was considerably easier to design and build TRI-RADIAL sails—spinnakers with several horizontal panels separating the head and clew region (Figure 8.2f).

In the past five years the tri-radial spinnaker has assumed a position of overwhelming dominance. Larger racing boats carry spinnaker inventories of half a dozen or more—all tri-radial designs. Few sailmakers now recommend horizontal or radial head sails for any racing boats larger than dinghys. Nowadays, the only common application of horizontal (or vertical) panel construction in spinnakers is for asymmetrical cruising spinnakers where economy of construction is sometimes considered more important than shape-holding ability.

Most refinements in tri-radial spinnaker design are currently being made in the bottom region, from the lower horizontal panel down to the foot itself. The bottoms of most early tri-radials consisted of two completely flat radial clews built from straight-sided triangular panels. These clews were joined together at the midline of the spinnaker by a shaped miter seam—the only broadseaming anywhere below the horizontals. Under load, the bottoms of flat clew tri-radials tend to become W-shaped in cross section, a fault known as clew inversion. To avoid it, sailmakers are introducing convexity into the edges of the clew panels to give the clews themselves some three-dimensional shape, as well as refining the shape of the curves at the edges of the miter seam.

SPINNAKER CONSTRUCTION

Compared to working sail construction, a great deal of cloth is inevitably wasted building triradial spinnakers. Fortunately, spinnaker cloths are less expensive than polyester sailcloths. Spinnaker panels are normally cut in stacks of five to seven layers—the maximum number that can be separated conveniently after being cut with an electric hotknife. Head panels are often all cut to one pattern, although sophisticated designs usually employ several. Horizontals are generally all cut together in one stack, as are clew panels.

After cutting, the panels of a spinnaker are sewn together to form four separate sections: the head, the joined horizontals, and the two clews. This is a time-consuming process because of the large number of panels in modern spinnakers. Spinnaker seams are almost never taped together in advance. Some machine operators use seaming guides, but most depend upon skill and experience to maintain seam uniformity. A two-step sewing machine is frequently used for spinnaker seaming as a time-saving measure. If a normal zigzag stitch is employed, two passes are required to provide adequate seam strength.

Once the head, horizontals, and clews are assembled, the edges where they will join each other are trimmed. The curvature of these edges has a major effect upon final sail shape. Because they have a great deal of three-dimensional shape, radial heads must be fanned in order to flatten the lower edge enough to permit accurate trimming.

At this point, the four sections of the spinnaker are assembled. Now the sail is ready for final trimming—the equivalent of second layout for a working sail. First, maximum half girths for the finished sail are measured from the existing midline marks and marked near the still untrimmed leeches. Next, one leech is fanned and a strip of material thirty to sixty centimeters wide is carefully pinned flat to the floor. Using the maximum half girths as a guide, the sailmaker bends a long batten around a series of pins to fair in a suitable leech curve. In general, spinnaker leech curves, as seen on the loft floor, are a combination of concave and nearly straight sections (Figure 8.3). Convex leeches are usually unstable. Once satisfied with a curve, the sailmaker trims the edge of the sail with an electric hot-knife using the edge of the batten as a guide. The sailmaker now trims the other leech, taking pains to make the sail symmetrical, except in the case of cruising spinnakers. Similar technique is used to trim the foot.

Now the spinnaker is ready for finishing. First, patches are constructed using multiple layers of three and a half or four and a half ounce polyester sailcloth in most cases, with cover patches of appropriately colored spinnaker nylon. Spinnaker patches must be large because the lightweight cloth used for the bodies of spinnakers is incapable of withstanding the concentrated loads near the corners of these

Figure 8.3
Spinnaker leech curves ordinarily consist of a combination of concave and nearly straight sections. Sailmakers' pins are used to spring a lofting batten to the desired shape.

sails without substantial reinforcement. The edges of spinnaker patches often have a jagged outline to reduce the risk of the entire patch tearing out of the sail.

The edges of most spinnakers are taped, using colored nylon tape. The weight of the tape selected normally ranges from one and a half to three ounces and depends on the size and application of the spinnaker. As with other sails, having the correct amount of tension on the tape as it is sewn to the sail is critically important. Too little tension makes for slack, unstable leeches and a floppy foot. Too much results in hooked leeches and excessive fullness.

The only handwork ordinarily involved in spinnaker construction is placing rings at the three corners. Very large spinnakers sometimes sport webbing straps to reinforce these rings.

9 Sail Trimming

EVEN if your actual sailing experience is quite limited, at this point you should have a pretty good idea of how to set and adjust sails correctly, simply from having read this far. The purpose of this chapter is to summarize the methods commonly used to adjust camber, camber distribution, and twist while actually sailing. Since this is a book about basic, not advanced, sailing techniques, I will not attempt to explain how to adjust sail shape to deliver maximum speed in every sort of boat and sailing condition. I will, however, devote extra attention to the methods used to alter the three-dimensional shape of spinnakers, because many sailors seem to find this confusing.

GOOD HEADSAIL TRIM

The position of the headsail sheet lead on deck is critical because it determines first, the LEAD ANGLE or angle between the headsail sheet and the horizontal plane, and second, the so-called SHEETING ANGLE or angle between the foot of the sail and the centerline of the boat (Figure 9.1). Let's look at the importance of each of these variables one at a time.

The intersection angle of the headsail sheet with the clew

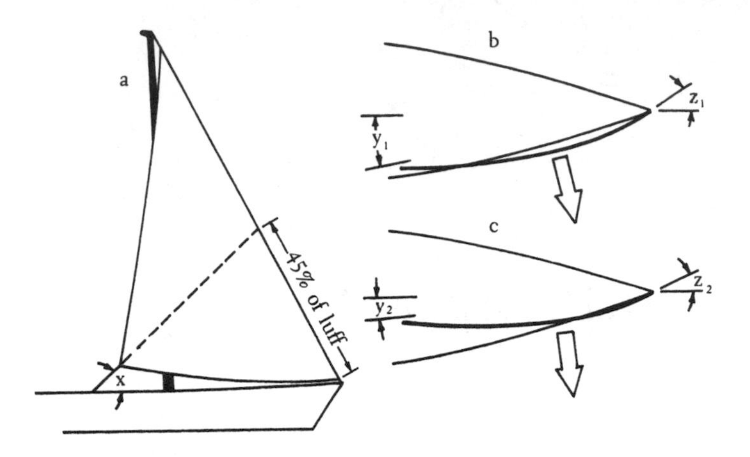

Figure 9.1
A sheet lead position generating a good average lead angle (angle x) can be estimated by projecting a line from a point 45 percent of the luff length above the tack as shown in diagram a. All else being equal, a larger sheeting angle (angle y_1) shown in diagram b produces a larger entry angle (angle z_1) than the smaller sheeting angle y_2 shown in diagram c.

determines the ratio of downward to backward forces that the sheet imposes upon the sail. A more downward, less backward pull tightens the leech which reduces twist and adds camber, especially near the head. At the same time it permits the clew to move forward, closer to the tack, which causes the foot of the sail to become fuller (Figure 9.2a). Thus if a fuller sail is desired and a reduction in twist can be tolerated, a simple solution is moving the headsail lead forward to make the vertical lead angle steeper, while continuing to use the same amount of sheet tension. The same effect can be achieved by repositioning the tack of the sail farther above the stem of the boat through the use of a tack pennant.

Conversely, a less downward, more backward pull on the headsail sheet allows the sail to twist more while reducing camber in the foot (Figure 9.2b). Twist is increased and camber throughout the sail is somewhat reduced. This is

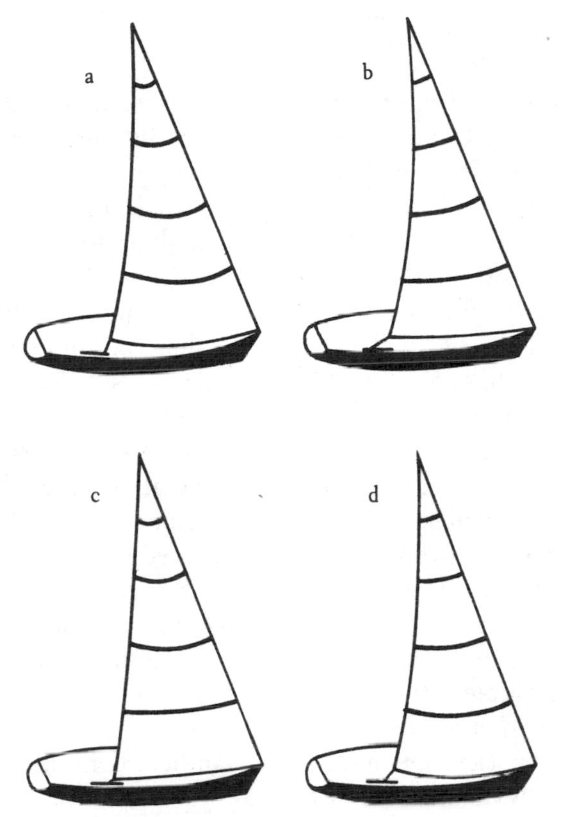

Figure 9.2
Effects of altering headsail sheet lead angle: With the lead forward, sail is full from head to foot and twist is minimized (a), with the lead aft it is flattened throughout and more twisted (b). Altering sheet tension has related, but different, consequences: More sheet tension flattens the foot, but reduces twist and increases camber near the head (c); less sheet tension increases camber near the foot while allowing the head to twist away and flatten (d).

normally accomplished by moving the headsail sheet lead aft.

A good rule of thumb for approximating the vertical lead angle involves marking a point on the luff that is 45 percent of the luff length above the tack, and extending a line from that point, through the clew, and on to its intersection with the deck or cabin top (Figure 9.1a). In most cases, that intersection point will be close to an optimal lead position.

The headsail sheeting angle, or "lead angle" as viewed from above, affects both the entry angle of the sail and the ratio of forward to lateral lifting forces generated by the sail. Thus when the headsail lead is moved inboard, the entry angle of the headsail becomes smaller, permitting higher pointing (Figure 9.1b). On the negative side, a more inboard lead causes the net lifting force produced by the sail to be directed more to the side. Propulsive force decreases and the heeling force increases. In general, smaller sheeting angles (inboard leads) are appropriate for smooth water beating where relatively less power is needed to propel the boat and accurate steering is practical. Rough water calls for wider lead angles to provide drive and a more forgiving helm (Figure 9.1c). On any sort of reach, the widest lead angle possible within the confines of the deck is appropriate for most monohulls.

SHEET TENSION affects the camber of headsails a bit differently than lead adjustment does. Increasing sheet tension moves the clew both back and down. This makes the foot of the sail flatter, while simultaneously closing the leech, which reduces twist and increases camber near the head of the sail (Figure 9.2c). Naturally, easing the headsail sheet has the opposite effect (Figure 9.2d).

The consequences of varying luff sag were introduced in Chapter 4. To recap the main points, more luff sag increases headsail camber and moves the position of maximum depth farther forward, particularly near the head. Less luff sag has the opposite effect. The principal trimming controls used to alter headsail luff sag while underway are the masthead backstay, and in the case of fraction rigs, the running backstays. Mainsail leech tension also plays a role,

Figure 9.3
In a sloop rig, tensioning the mainsail leech by hauling in mainsheet transmits tension to the headstay and reduces headstay sag.

particularly in smaller boats (Figure 9.3).

Varying luff sag also has an effect on twist (Figure 9.4). When the luff sags, it moves to leeward more than the leech. The result is a reduction in twist because, like the other effects of luff sag, the effect is most pronounced near the head where the overall girth of the sail is comparatively small.

As we know already from Chapters 4 and 5, increasing the luff tension on a headsail moves the position of maximum depth forward by stretching the sailcloth in the luff on the bias (see Figure 5.5). The entry of the headsail becomes rounder and its entry angle increases, making the sail become more forgiving at the expense of some pointing ability. Again, easing the halyard has exactly the opposite effect.

Since headsail luff tension is normally increased by rais-

Figure 9.4
When the headstay sags, the luff of the headsail moves aft and to leeward. The result is an increase in headsail camber, particularly near the head, accompanied by a small reduction in twist.

ing the head of the sail with the halyard, this adjustment also has a secondary effect that is frequently overlooked. When the head of the sail moves up, leech tension as well as luff tension increases, twist is reduced, and the sail becomes fuller toward its head. Of course, if the luff is tensioned by pulling down on a CUNNINGHAM CRINGLE set a short distance up the luff, the leech tension will not be affected.

Headsail trim is assessed, first and foremost by boat

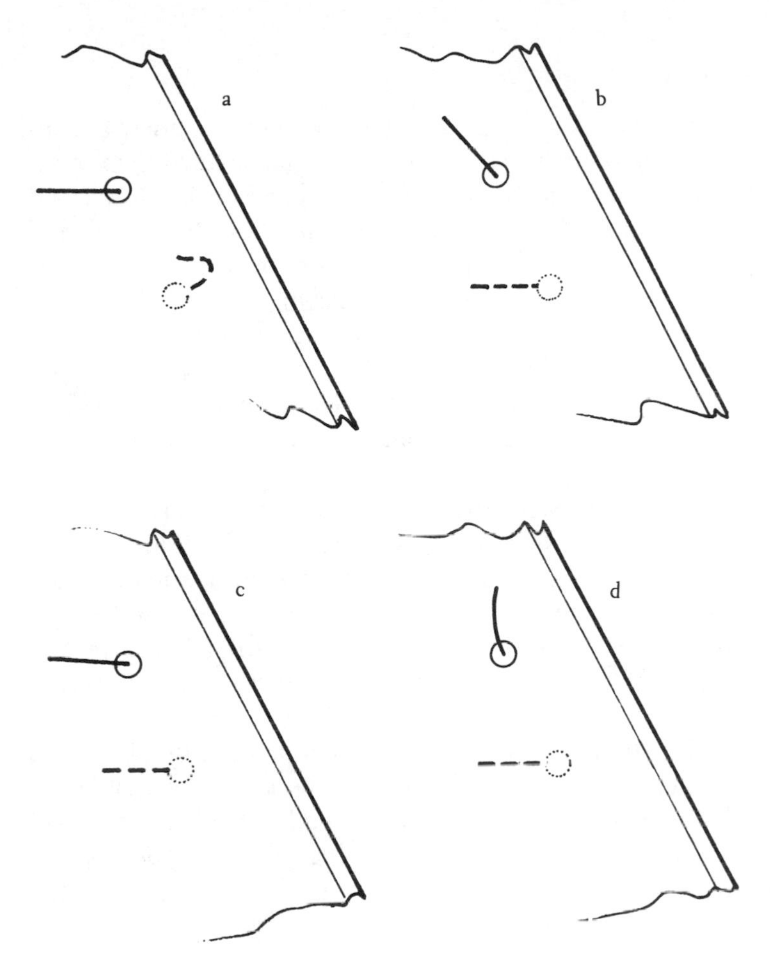

Figure 9.5
The telltales on the headsail luff are an invaluable help in achieving good upwind performance. If the leeward telltale (normally viewed through the sail) flutters (a), the sail is fully stalled and the boat must be brought up to course immediately. With both telltales extending straight aft (b), the boat is footing. Use this setting for punching through waves and close reaching. When the windward telltale angles upward, but streams smoothly (c), the boat is "feathering up." Steeper telltale angles indicate higher pointing which is appropriate for smooth seas. However, if the windward telltale extends straight up and becomes unstable (d), the boat is being pinched too much and the headsail is starting to luff.

performance, and secondarily by positioning clues, the appearance of draft stripes, and telltale behavior. Useful positioning clues include the distance between the leech and the spreader tip(s), as well as scales for sheet lead and halyard tension adjustments. A series of two or three horizontal draft strips in a dark, contrasting color make it easier to estimate the camber and camber distribution. Ideally headsails should be examined from a vantage point forward of the shrouds. Viewed from the cockpit, the position of maximum depth appears farther aft than is actually the case.

Pairs of telltales should be positioned at intervals up the port and starboard sides of the headsail luff as described in Chapter 3. When all the telltales luff simultaneously, the entry angle and, in the case of a well-designed sail, the twist as well, is correctly adjusted. Optimum upwind performance for most modern boats in smooth seas is achieved with the windward telltales streaming smoothly back but angled substantially above the horizontal (Figure 9.5). The telltales angle upward in this way because crossflow is induced by the aft slope of the headsail luff. Helmsmen find this a valuable indicator of how high they are pointing the boat.

GOOD MAINSAIL TRIM

Adjusting the flying shape of the mainsail appropriately is easier than trimming a headsail, partly because the mainsail is easier to see, and partly because its controls are more positive and produce fewer mixed effects. Nevertheless, the principles involved are basically the same.

The sheeting angle of a mainsail is altered by adjusting the angle of the main boom with respect to the centerline of the boat. In most cases this is done by repositioning the traveler car while sailing upwind and by easing or hauling

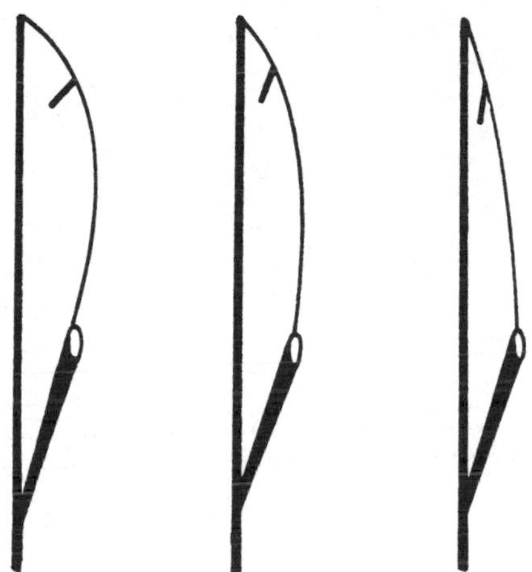

Figure 9.6
Twist in most mainsails is readily judged by looking at the angle made by the top batten with respect to the boom. For most conditions, twist is correct when the top batten is parallel to the boom (middle). If twist is excessive, the batten points off to leeward (left), while if the leech is too tight it pokes to windward (right).

in mainsheet while reaching. Since most mainsails are situated in the downwash of headsails, satisfactory sheeting angles are generally six to eight degrees smaller than the corresponding headsail lead angles.

Twist in a mainsail is controlled by leech tension and mast bend (the analog of luff sag in a headsail). The angle between the main boom and the top batten provides a good visual check for mainsail twist. When the two are parallel, the twist is close to optimal for most boats and most conditions (Figure 9.6). While sailing upwind, twist is normally controlled using mainsheet tension and the mast bending controls if there are any. On reaches, when the boom is swung outboard, twist is adjusted with the vang.

Camber in the lower third of a mainsail is adjusted with the clew outhaul which simply alters the distance between clew and the tack. On mainsails that are equipped with a flattening reef, the flattening reef tackle simply behaves like

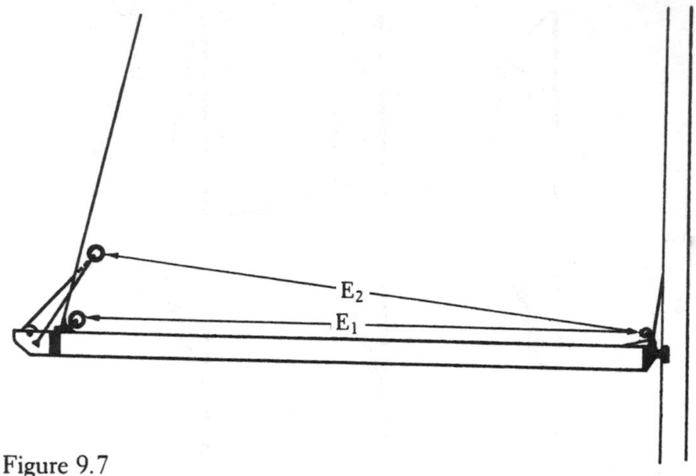

Figure 9.7
A flattening reef in the foot of a main is really just an extension of the outhaul adjustment. Since distance E_2 is less than distance E_1, when the flat reef cringle is hauled out to the black limiting band on the boom the cloth along the foot is additionally tensioned. The effect is the same as pulling the normal clew out past the black band.

an outhaul with a greater ranger of travel than the length of the boom (or the constraints of a race measurement rule) would otherwise permit. Figure 9.7 illustrates how a flattening reef works.

Camber in the upper two thirds of a mainsail is controlled by luff curvature and leech tension just as in the case of a headsail. In boats where mast bend can be adjusted, the controls normally used are backstays, babystays, and sometimes the forward thrust from a powerful boom vang. Leech tension is again adjusted with the mainsheet or the vang on beats and reaches respectively.

The position of maximum draft in mainsails is again controlled by adjusting luff tension. A Cunningham tackle rigged to a Cunningham cringle fifteen to thirty centimeters above the tack is the most common adjusting device.

The most useful position for a telltale anywhere on the mainsail is on the upper leech near the outer end of the top batten. When this telltale is streaming aft, it indicates that the sail is flat enough aloft and twisted sufficiently not to stall. On the other hand, when the telltale lifts and flutters continuously, camber should be reduced toward the top of the sail and twist increased. The maximum useful power for light and moderate conditions is usually generated when the upper leech telltale on the main lifts about half the time.

TRIMMING THE HEADSAIL AND MAINSAIL TOGETHER

Aerodynamically, the headsail and mainsail behave as a unit, so a good sailing crew treats them as such. At the ultimate level, this means that every trim adjustment of one sail should be matched with an appropriate trim adjustment of the other. To discuss these procedures in detail would be beyond the scope of this book, but I will mention a few points.

Mainsail backwinding, a common complaint of sailors, can be caused by a main that is built too full. More often, however, it results from improper main and headsail trim. The lower third of mainsails used with large overlapping genoas should be quite flat. Use plenty of outhaul—too much rather than too little if in doubt. The draft of a mainsail set with an overlapping headsail must be close to 50 percent aft to avert backwinding, so be sure the luff tension is not excessive. Finally, don't oversheet the headsail or attempt to use too small a headsail sheeting angle.

Different rig configurations require that the component sails be set up with differing amounts of twist. Compare a masthead sloop to its fractionally rigged counterpart. Figure 9.8 illustrates how both the headsail and the main of the fractional rig must be trimmed with substantially more twist than the masthead sails. This must be done because a fractional rig headsail tapers much more quickly than the mainsail set behind it, whereas a masthead headsail tapers at

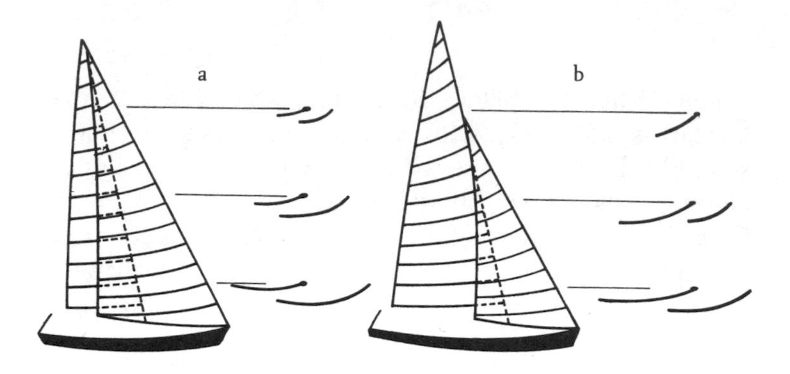

Figure 9.8
Both the headsail and mainsail of a masthead rigged sloop (left) should have less twist than their fractional rig counterparts (right) because both sails of the masthead rig taper at about the same rate whereas those of the fractional rig do not. Consequently, the upwash and downwash interactions of the two sails in the masthead rig are uniform from top to bottom, while in the fractional rig they vary from height to height.

about the same rate as its main. Near deck level in both rigs, the headsail creates a substantial downwash around the main which in turn produces a proportionally potent upwash for the benefit of the headsail. A more or less constant ratio of upwash and downwash effects extends all the way up to the top of a masthead rig. On the other hand, near the top of the foretriangle of a fractional rig, the upwash induced by the broad expanse of mainsail at that level causes a dramatic "lift" where the relatively narrow upper portion of the headsail is situated. Since the headsail is narrow at that height, the downwash it produces is very modest, so the middle of the main operates in wind that is substantially lifted relative to the apparent wind angle in the strong downwash zone farther below. Above the foretriangle, the mainsail is essentially a cat mainsail, and the apparent wind is still farther abeam. Accordingly the mainsail of a fractional rig, as well as the headsail must be twisted considerably in excess of their masthead brethren.

For most sloops, and particularly masthead rigged ones, it is quite valid to regard the headsail as the primary propulsive unit. The mainsail provides upwash to "supercharge" the headsail, and permits the helm balance and total heeling force to be quickly and conveniently adjusted.

TRIMMING A SPINNAKER

Spinnakers respond to trim adjustments in fundamentally the same ways as mains and headsails. The basic rule of sail shape again applies: anything that causes leech and luff to move closer to one another will make the sail fuller, or conversely, anything that causes leech and luff to separate will flatten the sail.

A stronger downward pull on the spinnaker leech will reduce the tendency of the upper leech regions to fall away to leeward. Similarly more downward pull on the spinnaker luff (or windward "leech" if you really prefer such confusing

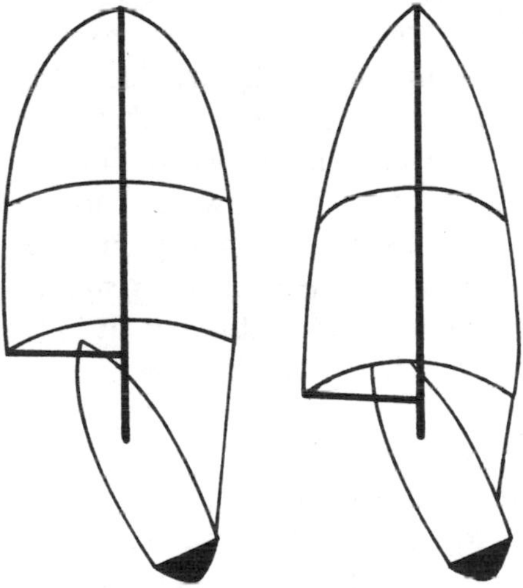

Figure 9.9
Lowering the pole and moving the sheet lead forward (right) causes the luff and leech of a spinnaker to hook inward. Overall camber increases.

terminology) causes the upper luff to hook to windward. In either case the edges of the sail move closer together and the overall fullness of the spinnaker increases. On a conventional or racing type spinnaker, these two adjustments are performed by lowering the pole and moving the sheet lead forward (Figure 9.9). For a cruising spinnaker they are accomplished by shortening the tack pennant and again moving the sheet lead forward.

On the other hand, allowing the tack and clew to rise allows the edges of the spinnaker to spread apart, reducing camber. Since most modern tri-radial spinnakers are deliberately built flat for close reaching, it is often desirable to trim for maximum camber while broadreaching and running. This can be achieved only by deliberately tensioning the luff and leech (i.e. setting the pole low and moving the sheet lead far forward). It should be noted that easing the spinnaker halyard has much the same effect as allowing the luff and clew to rise: luff and leech tension are reduced causing the spinnaker to become flatter.

As with other sails, the position of maximum depth of a spinnaker can be altered through trim adjustments. Lowering the pole without simultaneously altering the sheet lead position causes the luff to hook inward more than the leech, creating a fuller, more draft-forward shape (Figure 9.10). Conversely, more leech tension without a corresponding decrease in pole height yields a fuller spinnaker with the position of maximum draft farther aft. It follows that on a reach, contrary to a fairly popular belief, the tack of a spinnaker should be lower than the clew to produce a rounded entry and a nice open leech.

The alterations in spinnaker leech and luff tension discussed up to this point affect the upper portions of the sails—the shoulders—far more than the tack and clew areas. On the lower third of the sail, camber is controlled

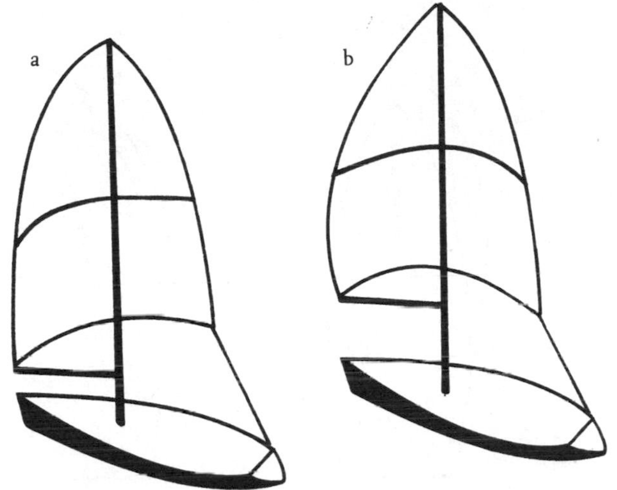

Figure 9.10
By lowering the spinnaker pole on a reach (left), the luff is tightened without affecting the leech. The result is a more draft-forward, genoa-like shape. Raising the pole (right) moves the maximum depth position aft. The flat entry makes the sail temperamental, and in most cases, the rounded leech area creates excessive drag.

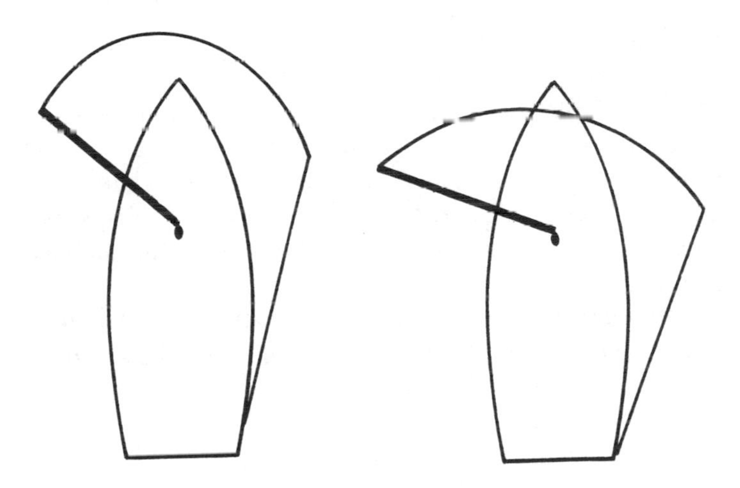

Figure 9.11
With the pole forward and the spinnaker sheeted correctly (on edge), the bottom half of the sail will be fuller than with the pole further aft.

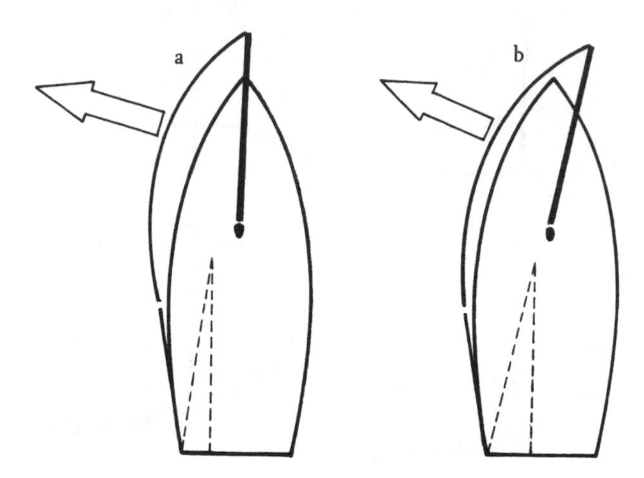

Figure 9.12
"Oversquaring" the pole (right) on a spinnaker reach widens the lead angle by moving the tack to windward. As a result, the net lifting force generated by the sail is rotated to a more forward direction. The boat heels less and goes faster, although it cannot pinch quite so high.

predominantly by changing the distance between tack and clew just as with other sails. If the pole is swung forward and the sheet eased enough to maintain the spinnaker "on edge," the foot of the sail will become fuller (Figure 9.11). On the other hand, if the outer end of the pole is hauled aft, and the sheet pulled in sufficiently to prevent a collapse, the tack and clew are drawn apart and the foot of the spinnaker gets flatter.

The sheeting angle of a spinnaker is also altered when the pole is swung forward or aft. Reaching under the spinnaker on a monohull with the apparent wind forward of the beam, it is usually impossible to open the sheeting angle sufficiently, because the deck beam aft is excessively narrow. However, the same effect can be achieved by "oversquaring" the spinnaker pole, hauling it aft a short distance so it no longer contacts the headstay (Figure 9.12).

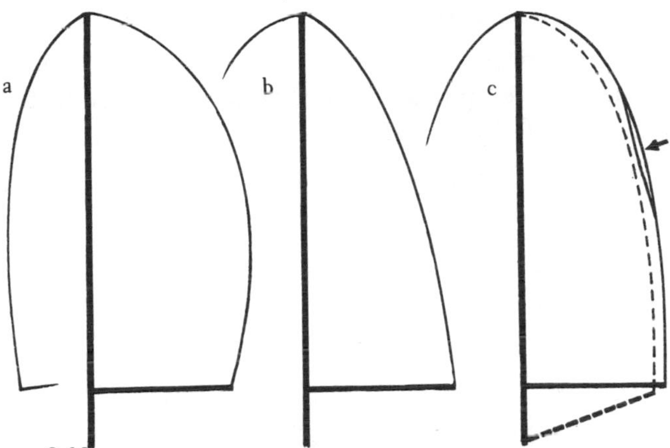

Figure 9.13
Optimal fore-and-aft pole position is indicated when the luff of the spinnaker (sheeted correctly so it is just ready to curl) rises vertically from the end of the spinnaker pole (right). If it angles to windward (left), the pole is too far forward. If it angles to leeward (middle), the pole is too far aft. After the fore-and-aft position of the pole is correctly set, the height of the pole can be adjusted by checking where the luff folds or breaks first when the spinnaker sheet is eased. Optimal pole height generally produces a break about 60 percent of the luff length above the tack (arrow). If the break is higher, the pole is low and vice versa.

There are a few key indicators for proper trim in a modern tri-radial spinnaker. As a means of determining the correct fore-and-aft pole position, look at the way the luff of the spinnaker rises from the pole end when the sheet is eased until the luff is just about ready to curl. If it slopes to leeward, the pole is too far aft (Figure 9.13b); but if it slopes to windward, the pole is too far forward (Figure 9.13a).

Once the fore-and-aft angle of the pole is essentially correct, select the proper pole height by watching where the spinnaker luff curls first. If it begins to fold close to the tack and the entire sail collapses immediately afterward, the pole is too high. On the other hand, if it folds first near the head, and tolerates an extravagant amount of luff curl before collapsing, the pole is too low. Ideally, the luff should curl first about 60 percent of its length above the tack (Figure 9.13c). Incidentally, the spinnaker pole should always project perpendicularly from the mast. If it does not, valuable projected area is lost.

10 Maintenance, Repairs, and Alterations

SAILS change with age, in most cases for the worse. Some aren't very good to begin with as a result of poor sailcloth, construction defects, or errors in design. Often improvements can readily be achieved, but some would be too difficult and costly to seriously contemplate. For a sailor who wishes either to maintain an existing sail inventory or to enlarge it through the purchase of used sails, it is important to know something about sail maintenance and the correction of sail faults.

SAIL CARE

Modern synthetic sails require a great deal less attention than cotton ones did, but they are not completely maintenance free. It's a good idea to inspect regularly for mechanical damage. Simply looking closely at sails aloft and inspecting them carefully while folding and bagging will catch most problems at an early stage.

If possible, sails should be dried before storage. Salty ones should be rinsed with fresh water because salt deposits attract moisture from the atmosphere, making sails heavier and more prone to mildew. Although fungi such as mildew live only on surface contaminants and do not attack the sailcloth itself, most people prefer to do without them. The dyes used for spinnaker cloth are not always completely colorfast, and have been known to run if stored wet for prolonged periods.

Dirty sails can be carefully washed with mild detergent and cold or lukewarm water. Cautious tumble drying at low heat settings is OK for spinnakers, but electric ironing is an extremely poor idea. Oily or greasy stains can safely be removed with a solvent such as mineral spirits. Rust stains on polyester sails respond to a 5 percent oxalic acid solution which at the same time bleaches the cloth. Bloodstains can be removed with mild ammonia solutions and mildew with dilute chlorine bleach. After using any of these cleaning agents, wash and thoroughly rinse the treated area.

Sharp points and edges are a major threat to sails, particularly for easily torn fabrics such as resin coated polyesters or Mylar® laminates. It's a good idea to go inch by inch over the deck and rig periodically, covering all potential hazards with plastic tape. In addition, the leeches of overlapping genoas should be protected by fabric chafe patches. It is best to position these patches by hoisting the sail and marking the actual point of spreader tip contact. Attempting to position spreader patches on a new sail using a sail plan generally involves too much guesswork.

HOLES AND CHAFE DAMAGE

Day to day wear and tear on sails most commonly takes its toll in the form of small rips, perforations, and worn spots. Stitching, since it stands above the level of the sailcloth itself, is particularly vulnerable to chafe and deterioration caused by the ultraviolet component in sunlight.

Small defects in the body of a sail that do not extend

across a seam are readily repaired. The basic technique involves sewing a patch of a similar material over the damaged area prior to cutting away the old cloth beneath. Temporary repairs can be made, either by darning with a heavy needle and thread, or using adhesive-backed tapes. The latter method is extremely easy and entirely satisfactory, provided the damaged area is dry when the tape is applied. Sailmakers and chandleries sell spinnaker repair tape made of rip-stop nylon and insignia tape made of three-ounce polyester sailcloth that can be applied one or more layers thick to patch other sails.

Tears along seams or tablings, at the edges or end of batten pockets, and major rips anywhere in the sail all require special techniques and some skill to repair satisfactorily. Ambitious amateurs willing to buy the necessary tools can learn to do these jobs from any of several books on sailmaking techniques, but most will probably elect to take the problem to a sailmaker. Badly mutilated sails often turn out to be old, much weakened from years of weathering, and basically not worth the cost of repairs. If a tear in the cloth can be started by hand or extended with just a gentle tug, the sail is probably not worth saving. If such a sail is repaired, the old "rotten" cloth alongside the new, strong patch will probably fail shortly after the sail is returned to service. Roller furling headsails that lack protective sun covers (see Chapter XI) often suffer serious, and for most practical purposes, irreparable ultraviolet damage along a band down the leech and across the foot.

The condition of the stitching in the seams of a sail can be tested by hooking a pointed object under a thread and gently lifting. If the thread breaks readily, the stitching is weak and should be replaced. Restitching a sail is actually a simple operation provided the seams are still intact. Most customers are surprised by how little the average sailmaker charges for this job. A typical cruising sail is good for at least two restitching jobs before the sail itself bites the dust. The cloth in a racing sail generally gets "tired," causing the sail to lose its competitive edge before the stitching weakens seriously. However, if this sail is phased into a cruising role, it too will eventually become a candidate for restitching.

HARDWARE FAILURES

If properly selected and installed, sail hardware doesn't break. Of course, in reality hese items do fail from time to time, and some are more trouble prone than others. Mainsail slides and slugs, particularly those near the head and clew, are potential weak spots. It is good sailmaking practice to fit a long metal slug or a series of closely spaced metal slides at the head (Figure 10.1a). If the boom lacks an outhaul car, this should be done at the clew as well (Figure 10.1b). To rely on standard plastic fittings in these high load areas is asking for trouble.

Brass or plastic piston hanks occasionally will be worn through by the steel headstay, particularly if they are a little too small for the job. More commonly, the hanks chafe holes in the fabric near the luff of the sail. A visual inspection will quickly detect either problem. In addition, it's a good idea to lubricate piston hanks from time to time.

Unlike handworked rings, which usually deform before they tear out of the sail completely, modern pressed-in rings generally break away intact when stressed excessively, taking the entire corner of the sail with them. If a failure of this kind occurred while sailing, it would most likely indicate that the reinforcing patch at that corner of the sail was inadequate. An improperly installed ring generally can be detected by visual inspection. Excessive die pressure can crack parts of the ring, while insufficient pressure (or a

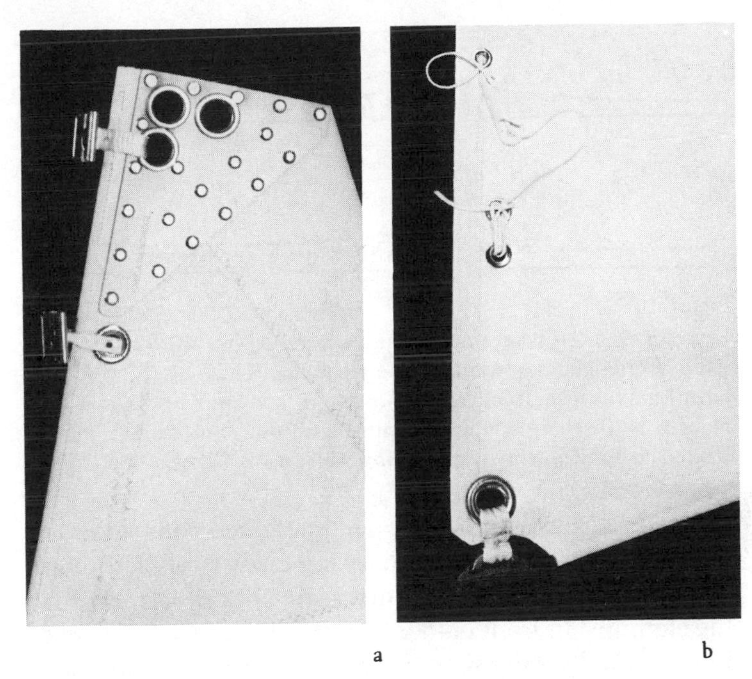

a b

Figure 10.1
In high load areas such as the head of this mainsail (a), slides or slugs should be placed close together. The nylon webbing used to attach the topmost slide is stronger and more flexible than a nylon shackle. Photograph b shows a mainsail with typical leechline cleating arrangement and an aluminum clew slug webbed to a pressed-in ring.

skimpy patch) will result in a ring that does not bite securely into the cloth.

HEADSAIL LEECH PROBLEMS

Building a smooth, stable leech on a sail without battens is one of the most difficult feats in sailmaking. I doubt that any sailmaker gets perfect leeches every time. Except in the case of some short-lived racing dinghy jibs where the leech is simply trimmed with a hot-knife and otherwise left un-

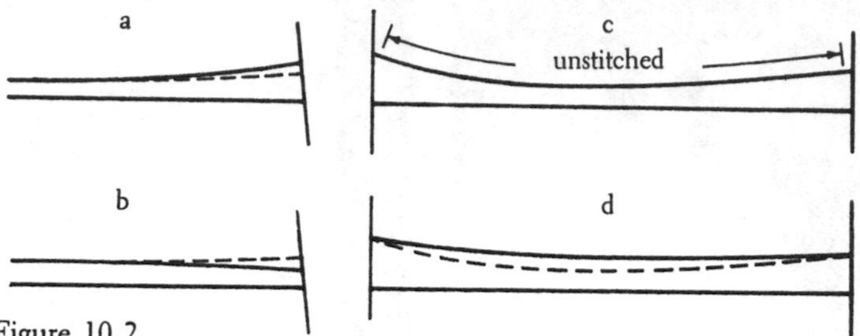

Figure 10.2
Diagram of a leech take-up (a) and a leech let-out (b). Dashed lines indicate original seam width. If the technique shown on the right, the broadseaming in a seam (shown in its original form in diagram c) is reduced by first unstitching the entire seam except at the luff and the leech; and subsequently reassembling with greater panel overlap (d).

finished, all headsail leeches are reinforced with some sort of tape or tabling. Since two or three layers of cloth comprise this leech reinforcement, it stretches much less than the cloth just in front of it. The result is a hooked or cupped leech, visually offensive and an impediment to air flow. Turbulence induced by the hook can make the leech flutter like a flag, shaking the entire sail and causing still more drag. Sails made of cloth that has, at some time, been loaded beyond its yield point are particularly prone to fluttery leeches.

To help combat these problems, almost all sailmakers trim the leeches of their headsails to a hollow or concave profile and enclose a LEECHLINE within the leech tabling. The leechline is ordinarily anchored at the head of the sail and leads through a grommet to a small cleat on one side of the clew patch (Figure 10.1b). Tensioning the leechline creates a drawstring effect, pulling aft against the concave leech tabling to stabilize the leech. Excessive leechline tension will, in itself, cause a leech to hook, so always use just barely enough to arrest leech flutter. The leechline should be eased completely when the sail is doused.

A headsail that lacks sufficient camber in the region just ahead of the leech will be prone to leech flutter. If this is the problem, a sailmaker can perform LEECH TAKE-UPS at the aft ends of a few seams (Figure 10.2). In addition to stabilizing the leech, this additional broadseaming will increase the total camber of the sail and move the average position of maximum depth further aft.

Another way to improve a slightly stretched or otherwise unstable leech is to retrim the leech to a more hollow or concave shape. This of course necessitates replacing the leech tabling, but can be worthwhile, particularly if the original leech hollow was insufficient.

Headsails with battens seldom have leech problems. Since they also lack a convex roach in most cases, batten troubles, as discussed in the following section, are also rare.

MAINSAIL LEECH PROBLEMS

Except for battenless, hollow-leeched cruising mains which have the same leech problems as battenless headsails do, most mainsail leeches give little trouble. When trouble does arise it generally stems from one of three sources: inadequate fill strength in the cloth selected; excessive roach for the batten length; or improper batten stiffness.

High aspect rigs and large moderate aspect ones put extremely high stresses on the leeches of their mainsails during beats in strong winds. Although battens do help to distribute the leech load uniformly across the leech section, it is still not uncommon to see mainsail leeches that stretch excessively and fall away to leeward when the wind pipes up. On cruising boats, increasing the lengths of some or all of the battens (and batten pockets, of course) can help somewhat. On racing boats, where the maximum length of battens is, in most cases, restricted, this treatment is out of bounds. The only real answer lies in selecting more robust cloth for the next mainsail.

The symptoms of excessive roach relative to batten length resemble those of excessive leech stretch as just described. Whenever the amount of roach extending beyond the straight line from head to clew is close to half the length of the battens, it tends to behave like a teeter-totter, causing the leech to become extremely unstable. Leech take-ups (more broadseaming), different battens, and less roach can all improve the situation. Leech take-ups are a cheap, easy way to stabilize a roach, but are appropriate only if the additional broadseaming will not make the sail excessively full and draft aft. Slightly longer battens inserted in the existing pockets will tend to bow under compression, supporting the roach a bit better than their predecessors in some cases. Likewise a stiffer set of battens can help a little. Fitting new batten pockets to accept longer battens works well, when the rules permit. As a last resort, the batten pockets can be relocated farther forward, the roach trimmed down, and the entire leech reconstructed at the cost of some sail area and a healthy chunk of sailmaking time.

Inappropriate batten stiffness frequently causes shape faults in mainsails. Toward the head, where the battens traverse a significant proportion of the total girth of the sail, battens should be tapered or otherwise graduated in stiffness, so that the more flexible end is farthest from the leech. This is most important for the top batten, but it is best to taper the next one down also. If the top batten is too stiff at the inboard end a hard spot will form there, giving the sail a V-shaped cross section in the head region. If the top batten is too flexible, it will bend excessively and the head will be too full and too draft aft. Different top battens may be needed to achieve optimal sail shape in various wind conditions.

EXCESSIVE FOOT ROACH

Foot roach (foot round) can be a source of extra unmeasured sail area in headsails and spinnakers. In addition, headsails that achieve good contact with the foredeck gain efficiency as a result of the end-plate effect (see Chapter 3). As a result, sailmakers sometimes attempt to squeeze more foot roach into these sails than is prudent. Foot roach is supported primarily by broadseams that introduce a considerable amount of three-dimensional shaping into the localized foot area. Using battens to support foot roach is impractical and/or illegal. Many sailmakers fit FOOTLINES, the analogs of leechlines, in their headsails. However, since the foot curve is convex and lacks battens to serve as struts to support the tensioned line, this approach actually contributes little to foot stability. Physical contact with the deck will steady a genoa foot to some extent, but if it flaps anyway, the only way to correct the problem is either to increase the take-up in the foot seams, or to trim back the foot roach itself.

SAILS THAT DON'T FIT RIGHT

Strange though it may seem, sailmakers have a lot of headaches ensuring that sails fit their customers' boats properly. The rigs of "stock" sailboats frequently evolve during a production run as a manufacturer refines the product or finds alternative sources of gear and fittings. Owners are sometimes unaware of changes that previous owners have made in a boat's rig. Frequently a sailmaker will be called upon to build sails for a new boat that is under construction only to find that the finished rig differs significantly from the yacht designer's drawings. Finally, of course, there are innumerable opportunities for measurement errors and

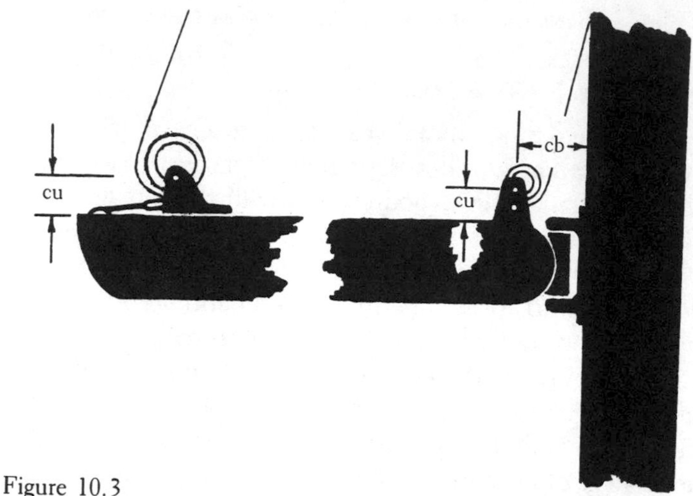

Figure 10.3
Tack and clew cut-up (CU) and tack cutback (CB). These measurements are normally taken from the top face of the boom or aft face of the mast to the bearing surface of the clevis pin or shackle that holds the tack or clew rig.

miscalculations in the sailmaking process.

Sails that are too big, for whatever reason, must be cut down enough to fit on the boat. This is usually quite feasible. It is much more difficult to enlarge sails that are too small. In a majority of cases, the most practical approach involves attaching additional panels to extend the foot downward (assuming crosscut construction), retrimming the luff, leech, and foot; and rebuilding the tablings and corner patches. To be worthwhile, the sail must be in good condition, and a sailcloth with properties that closely match those of the sail itself must be available for the new foot panels.

Sometimes the position of the bearing surface of the ring at the tack or clew or a sail does not correspond properly with the location of the clevis pin or hook at the bow fitting, gooseneck (fitting joining boom to mast), or outhaul car. If the tack ring is either too far aft or not aft enough, the sail is said to have too much cut-back or too little respectively (Figure 10.3). A corresponding error in the vertical placement of a tack or clew ring is an error in cut-up. To determine whether a particular set of wrinkles originating from the tack or clew of a sail are a result of one of these faults, remove the pin holding the appropriate ring in place and attempt to tie the ring into a more satisfactory alternative position. If this is possible, a sailmaker can relocate the permanent ring correctly, using what you have learned as a guide.

CAMBER FAULTS

Sails can be too full or too flat toward the top, toward the bottom, or all around. The draft can be located inappropriately, either in part of the sail or at all heights. To further complicate diagnosis, these faults can be caused, either by bad sail trim or by failings of the sail itself: excessive cloth stretch; inappropriate luff curves; or incorrect broadseam distribution. An overall understanding of the factors that determine flying sail shape as explained in Chapter 4, as well as familiarity with sail trimming techniques described in Chapter 9 will help a great deal in figuring out what you are up against. Of course, getting a sailmaker out on the boat for a look at the sail can help a lot too!

Once a camber fault is pinpointed, there are a battery of techniques, many already familiar to you, to improve the situation. Leech take-up or let-outs can, in most cases, be used to alter the camber anywhere in the aft half of the sail. The same technique can be used to alter the broadseam near the luff, but the luff tape and rope must be removed first, a difficult task on a sail equipped with slides or hanks.

Alternatively a seam can be unstitched for most of its length, but left intact at the luff and leech. If the amount of taper and the minimum seam overlap are now altered and the sail reassembled, the effect can be the same as a take-up or let-out at the ends of the seams (Figure 10.2 c and d).

To recut a luff curve, the luff tape is removed, the new curve faired and trimmed, and the sail reassembled. In most cases the amount of sail area lost is insignificant, although the sailmaking time required for the job can be substantial.

Of course sailmakers strive to get it right the first time because warranty work is inevitably a losing proposition. Most, however, will see a job through to a satisfactory conclusion. Major recutting and repair jobs at customers' expense are, for the most part, less of a bargain than they used to be, because the cost of sailmaking labor has increased faster than the cost of materials. Sailcloth never lasts forever, so a repair that costs nearly as much as a new sail makes little sense. Nevertheless, it is still not uncommon to find high quality older sails that can economically be given a new lease on life, or, by judicious rebuilding, altered for use on different boats.

11 Modern Sail-Handling Gear

A COMPREHENSIVE treatment of modern sail-handling gear would have to encompass all the variations in standing rigging, running rigging, and deck gear found on contemporary sailboats. Modern technology in the hands of keen sailors and inventors around the world has given birth to an incredible array of rigging options; ingenious and practical methods for handling sails. To do justice to this wealth of ideas would require a book in itself. I have picked out five classes of gear to discuss here: slab reefing systems; headstay foils; roller furling headsails; furling mains; and spinnaker caddies. All five are sufficiently new and important to justify discussion. In fact, these developments are profoundly changing the way yachts are crewed and handled.

SLAB REEFING

Slab reefing, also known as jiffy reefing or California reefing, has achieved almost universal acceptance among modern sailors, but the technique is still frequently misunderstood. At first glance, slab reefing resembles the traditional technique of tieing in a reef. However, the old method involved laboriously attaching the sail along the entire length of the boom, using a large number of closely spaced reef ties, while a slab reefed mainsail is anchored to the boom by only two lines, one from the reef tack and the other from the reef clew. Although slab reefing mainsails are usually provided with secondary reef ties toward the center of the sail, these must be used only to secure the loose folds of sailcloth to the boom once a slab has been pulled down. Before a slab reef is released, it is crucial to remove these ties. If they are permitted to sustain any sailing loads, the sail will probably tear.

The slab reefed main is sheeted just like a headsail. The REEF TACK is anchored firmly near the boom gooseneck just as the tack of a headsail is fixed to a deck fitting near the boat's stem. The OUTBOARD REEFING LINE acts like a headsail sheet in that it pulls aft and down on the clew. If the outboard reefing line is led to a point farther aft on the boom, the foot of the mainsail will be flattened just as the foot of a headsail will flatten if the sheet lead is moved farther aft. Alternatively, if the outboard reefing line is led farther forward, the foot of the main will become fuller. Outboard reefing lines are usually anchored at one end to the boom, pass through the reef clew ring, back to a cheek block on one side of the boom, and forward to a winch and/or cleat (Figure 11.1). If the attached end of the reefing line and this cheek block are positioned differently along the length of the boom, the effective lead angle will extend through a point halfway between the two.

The vertical lead angle for a reefed main becomes steeper (closer to vertical) as the outboard reefing line is eased. Thus if a fixed turning block for an outboard reefing line is accidentally attached to the boom behind the optimal location, little harm will be done, whereas if it is too far forward, it will prove impossible to flatten the foot of the reefed sail sufficiently.

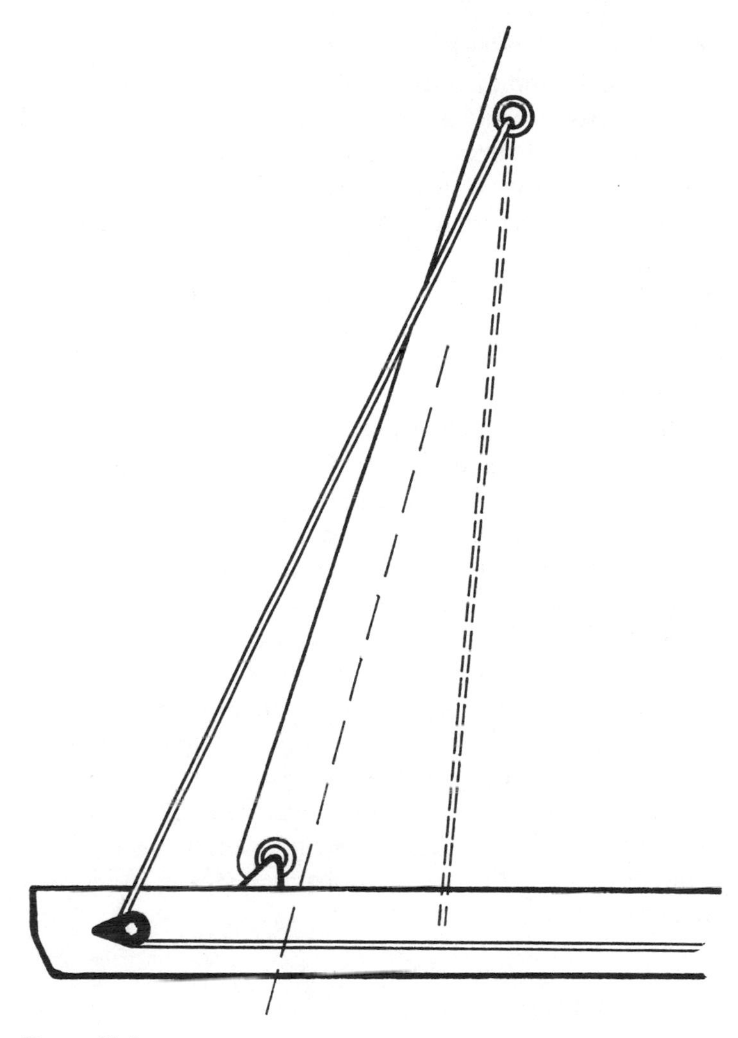

Figure 11.1
The outboard slab reefing line shown above extends up from an anchorage on the port side of the boom, through the reef clew ring, down to a turning block, and forward along the starboard side of the boom. Since the anchorage and the cheek block are located at different distances aft, the effective "lead angle" when the mainsail is reefed is shown by the dashed line.

The safest, most convenient slab reefing systems have separate forward and aft reefing lines for each reef, all lead aft to the cockpit. However, since many mainsails have two or even three reefs, a cumbersome and costly array of lines would be necessary to achieve this ideal. For this reason, it is more common to lead only the outboard reefing lines aft along the cabin top. The reefing tack selected is either slipped over a hook mounted on top of the gooseneck fitting, or is hauled down using an S-hook on the Cunningham tackle.

The reef tack and clew patches must sustain loads at least as great as those experienced by the corresponding reinforcements in the full-sized sail. This is a point to watch in evaluating sails, since reef patches are quite often, for whatever mysterious reasons, substantially smaller and less robust than the primary patches.

Slab reefing works quite well with headsails too, particularly high aspect jibs for heavy weather sailing. Since it is quite difficult, even dangerous, to attempt to retie a jib sheet to a flailing jib clew, it is a good idea to drop the sail completely to secure the slab. A disadvantage of reefing headsails is that the considerable weight of the reef clew patch(es) some distance up the leech makes the leech more prone to shake. In jibs with battens this is seldom a problem.

HEADSTAY FOIL SYSTEMS

Twin groove headstay foils have become standard equipment on ocean racing boats and racer/cruisers because they enable one headsail to be swapped for another without the devastating speed losses associated with sailing "bare headed." All headstay foils are plastic or aluminum extrusions containing two narrow-throated grooves to accept luff tapes with internal ropes. Most are hollow extrusions that slide or clip over an existing forestay. A few are continuous alloy members with sealed bearing assemblies at each end which substitute for a conventional forestay. One or more feeding devices at or near the bottom of the foil align and guide the luff tape through an opening or wide spot in one of the grooves as a sail is hauled up. When a sail change is required, the second sail is hauled up the vacant groove using a second halyard. After it is sheeted home, the first halyard is released and the original sail dropped and stowed.

Of course there are tricks to changing sails smoothly and easily. A battery of sophisticated techniques and equipment ranging from short sheets and special sausage bags to sail folding drills on the weather rail has evolved in the crucible of present-day big boat racing. These are thoroughly described in racing articles, books, and even educational films. They are too specialized to discuss here. Suffice to say: if scrupulous care is taken to avoid crossing the port and starboard headsail halyards, if the luff tapes of the headsails are correctly sized, and if the grooves of the headfoil and the luff tapes of the sail are frequently sprayed with a silicon fabric lubricant, major problems should not arise.

ROLLER LUFF HEADSAIL FURLING

There are two basic types of roller luff furling systems. The less sophisticated operates by wrapping the sail around its own internal luff wire (Figure 11.2a). More advanced gear roll the sail onto an aluminum alloy extrusion that either fits over the forestay or replaces it entirely (Figure 11.2b to d). Both types are turned from the bottom, either by unspooling a line from a drum, or by using a loop of line around a special corrugated sheave as a sort of belt drive.

Furling around an internal luff wire has several drawbacks. In order to operate, the sail must be completely independent of the boat's headstay. Thus the headstay lends no support to the luff. Even with a two-part halyard tackle, it is extremely difficult to obtain enough tension in the system to keep luff sag within reasonable limits. Excessive loads on the swivel at the top of the sail will, in some cases, cause it to bind.

Even the heftiest luff wires resist twisting forces quite poorly, which makes it difficult to reef successfully with a wire luff furling system. Sailing loads imposed by the half-furled sail often twist the luff wire, causing the top part of the furling wire to unwind a few turns and spoiling the shape of the sail.

Once constructed, it is impractical to adjust the luff tension on most wire luff furling sails because the fabric has been seized (lashed) tightly to the furling wire to prevent the wire from simply turning within the tape. This seizing also prevents the sail from sliding vertically over the luff tape when an alteration in maximum depth location is desired.

Furling systems that roll the sail onto an aluminum alloy extrusion avert all these problems. The extrusions used resemble the headstay foils mentioned earlier, although some have only a single groove. All are far more torsion resistant than wire ropes, primarily because of their greater diameters. There are a number of kits currently on the market that reversibly convert particular models of twin groove "racing type" headstay foils into roller furling systems. Since the extrusions twist very little along their lengths they can be readily used for roller reefing as well as for furling. Because the luff tape of the sail slides into a groove in the extrusion, it is practical to alter draft position by varying luff tension.

There are two sub-classes of extrusion type furling gear. The more common variety employs a head swivel mounted on a slider that runs over the outside of the extrusion (Figure 11.2b and c). Like the swivels used at the heads of wire

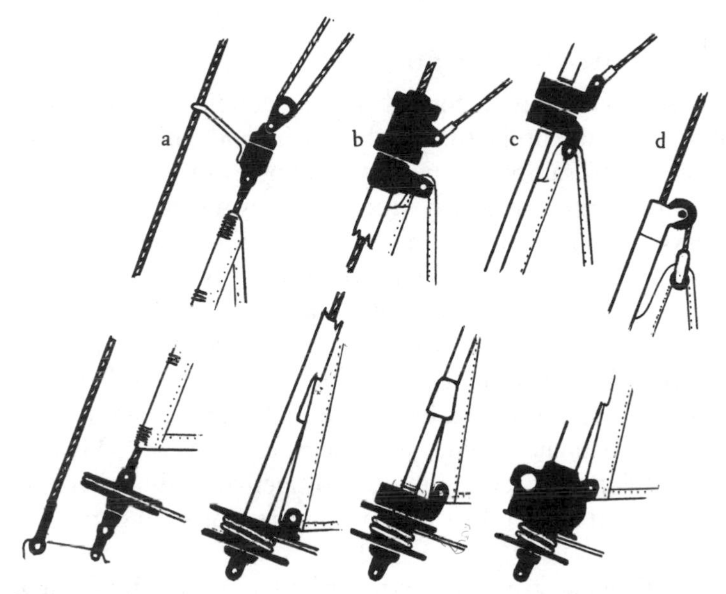

Figure 11.2
The most common types of headsail roller furling equipment: Diagram a shows a luff wire furling system with a two-part halyard attached to the head swivel and a single wrap furling drum. Diagram b depicts an extrusion-type furling gear fitted over a standard wire forestay. Diagram c shows a rotating extrusion that completely replaces the headstay. In this case, the swivels at the head and tack are designed so that the furling drum turns only the extrusion, causing the round near the center of the luff to be furled first. Diagram d represents a furling system with a self-contained halyard. The windlass for tensioning this halyard is attached to the top of the furling drum.

luff furling sails, its function is to prevent the halyard from either twisting or wrapping around the extrusion. The less popular variety of extrusion type furling gear has a self-contained halyard turning over a block mounted on the top of the extrusion in place of a head swivel (Figure 11.2d).

Although extrusion type furling equipment is sufficiently torsion resistant to function as headsail reefing gear, sail-making technology has only just recently neared the point where a single roller reefing headsail can be considered reasonably adequate for all sailing conditions. Basically there are two problems: cloth weight and sail shape. To build a headsail tough and stable enough for strong winds requires a robust sailcloth which basically means a relatively heavy sailcloth. Light wind sailing on the other hand requires lightweight sails that will fill easily. To reconcile these conflicting requirements in a single sailcloth is difficult, to say the least. Since a furling sail seldom needs to be lowered and bagged, it really does not need a soft hand; hence the selection of a heavily resinated fabric can help to provide adequate stability without excessive weight. Mylar® laminate furling sails also look attractive, although most cruising sailors tend to take a dim view of such a radical idea.

Vertical construction holds particular promise for furling sails because it permits step-up construction—the use of a stronger, but heavier sailcloth close to the leech (Figure 11.3a). When such a sail is reefed, lightweight cloth near the luff is the first to be rolled into furl.

A second obstacle to producing a satisfactory all-purpose furling headsail is providing satisfactory camber control. Sails that are full enough for light air become much too full as the luff sags and the sailcloth stretches in a stiff breeze. A recent refinement in roller furling equipment now offered by several manufacturers helps considerably to widen the effective wind range of furling headsails used with them. In the new gear, the head and tack of the sail are both attached to secondary swivels which permit the extrusion to rotate independently when furling begins. As a result, the first few turns of the drum remove convexity in the center of the luff curve without furling the head and tack. The effect is the same as recutting the sail with a more hollow luff—a reduction in the amount of draft that would otherwise be added as the headstay sags more in an increasing wind.

Despite these improvements, the owner or purchaser of a

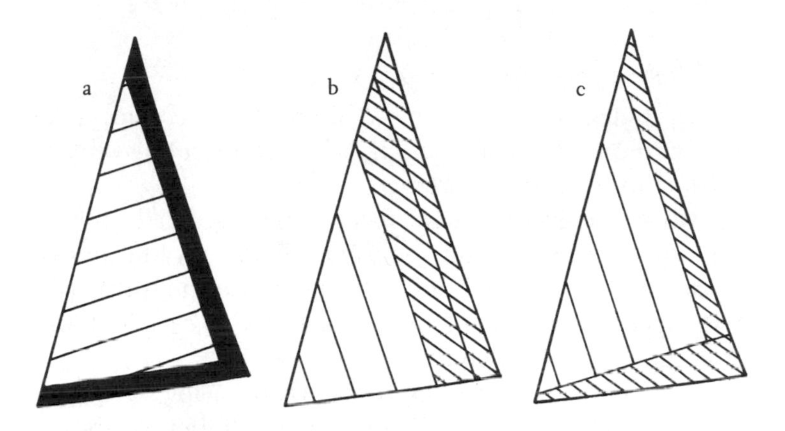

Figure 11.3
Protective sun strips are conventionally attached to the leech and foot of furling headsails as shown in a. Diagram b shows how vertical paneled step-up construction can be used to build a lighter furling genoa that still has relatively robust material in the leech area to withstand heavy weather sailing loads. If expensive ultraviolet resistant sailcloth is used in the leech and a special horizontal foot on a modified vertical panel sail (c), sewn-on sun strips can be eliminated.

headstay furling system should still seriously consider having more than one headsail. By purchasing two furling sails, a genoa for lighter winds and a jib for heavy going, the design of individual sails need be compromised less, and there is an extra sail in the inventory as insurance in case one gets damaged.

Sails that are furled on the headstay for storage must be protected from the weather. The most popular system involves sewing protective strips of material, usually about 40 cm (18″) wide down one side of the leech and the foot (Figure 11.3b). When the sail is rolled, these SUN STRIPS spiral around the outside of furl to cover the sail itself. Self-sacrificing sun strips are made of ordinary lightweight polyester sailcloth. These are the least expensive, but the shortest lived. Sun strips made of acrylic sail cover material provide a superior ultraviolet barrier and a choice of vivid colors, but cost plenty. In addition, their considerable weight injures the set of the sail, while contributing next to nothing to its stretch resistance.

Two alternatives to the sewn-on strip are separate protective LUFF SOCKS, and sun-resistant sailcloth. A luff sock is hoisted with a spare halyard and closed over the furled sail with zippers or patent fasteners. They provide excellent sun protection, but are inconvenient to use.

In recent years, extremely effective ultraviolet coatings have been developed for sailcloth, although they are somewhat costly. Vertical paneled furling genoas, if constructed with a horizontal foot, can be well protected by using expensive sun-resistant sailcloth for just the leech and foot areas (Figure 11.3c).

FURLING MAINSAILS

Although unlikely to rival the popularity of furling headsails, roller furling mains are gaining a following. There are two basic approaches: boom furling and luff furling.

Roller reefing, although popular before the advent of slab reefing, has some serious drawbacks. As a mainsail wraps like a roller blind around a rotating boom of uniform diameter, the luff and the leech wind on snugly, but the excess cloth in the "belly" of the sail has nowhere to go. Consequently, as the sail is furled further and further, its shape becomes increasingly distorted. Throwing sail bags and life jackets into the "pocket" as the reef is rolled in helps somewhat, but the practice lacks élan.

Recently a device consisting of four bowed rods that attach along the sides of a roller reefing boom has been marketed. The rods are adjusted to complement the camber of the mainsail so that the reef rolls on fairly smoothly. Possible stumbling blocks that remain are the risk of cloth over-

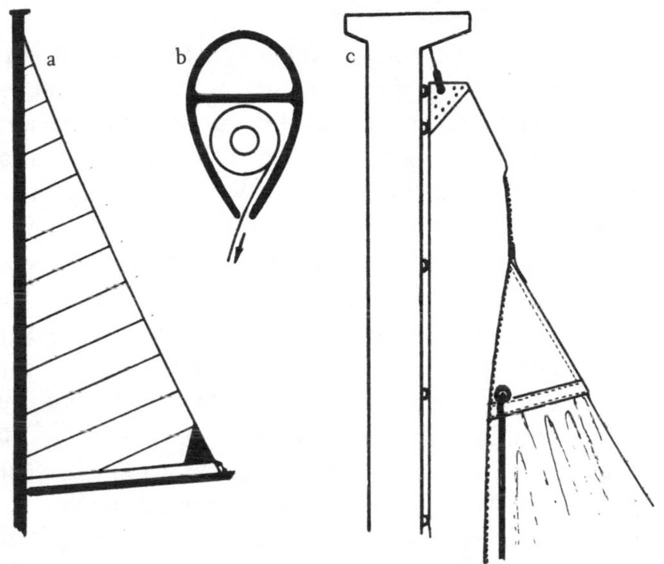

Figure 11.4
In-the-mast mainsail furling systems require a special, loose-footed, battenless mainsail with a smaller than normal tack angle (a). The mast sections used for in-the-mast furling (b) have a large aft compartment to house the furling gear. Zip Stop® mainsail furling (c), operates by pulling a zippered furling hood down from the head of the sail, compacting it into an integral storage sock. (In the diagram, the line for raising the furling hood is omitted for clarity.)

load in the "clew" area of the reefed sail for lack of any reinforcing patch, the difficulty of attaching a boom vang when reefed, and the cost of the gear itself. Nevertheless, the idea has promise.

The most basic and least satisfactory form of roller luff mainsail furling is simply a headsail type furling gear mounted vertically a short distance behind the mast. Luff sag in these systems causes the mainsail to become undesirably full in strong winds. Substantially reducing this sag by tensioning the furling system is difficult and greatly increases compression loading on the mast.

In-the-mast mainsail furling systems consist of a conventional furling gear contained within a special mast extrusion. The aluminum mast extrusions used have a longitudinal web dividing the section into separate front and rear compartments (Figure 11.4a). The furling gear is housed in the aft compartment which opens via a slit on the aft face of the mast to permit the sail to emerge. In use, the luff of the sail is supported laterally by the mast itself. These systems work well, but are bulkier, heavier, and more expensive than equivalent conventional masts.

Conventional mainsails work fine for roller boom furling, but those intended for either style of roller luff furling must be specially designed with a loose foot and a tack angle of less than 85° (Figure 11.4b). Of course, a convex roach supported by battens is out of the question. Instead a hollow leech like that of most headsails must be substituted with an attendant loss of sail area.

A third mainsail furling system currently marketed under the trade name Zip Stop® employs an entirely different and novel operating principle. A pair of zippers on each side of a modified, conventional mainsail guide a fabric hood over the head and down the length of the luff. As the furling hood is pulled down, the forward portion of the sail, which is sheathed in two layers of acrylic cover material, is inverted upon itself to form a tidy bag (Figure 11.4c). A Zip Stop® main currently costs about twice the price of a conventional one, but works on conventional masts and accepts battened sails. Although the device is new and relatively untested, it seems to work well.

SPINNAKER LAUNCHING AND RETRIEVING DEVICES

Since spinnakers have the reputation of being tough to handle, particularly in strong winds, a number of devices

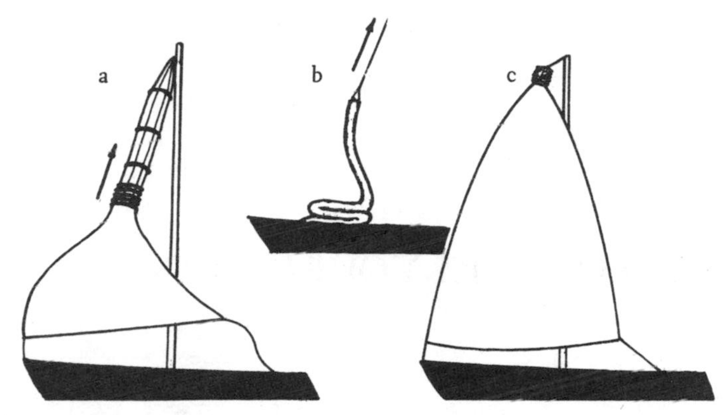

Figure 11.5
Spinnaker caddies all operate in much the same way. Diagram a shows an open caddie comprised of hoops lines being operated with its internal halyard to release the spinnaker. Diagram b shows a tube-type caddie with the spinnaker enclosed being hoisted on the spinnaker halyard. In diagram c, the spinnaker is flying, and the caddie shown in b is corrugated at the head of the sail.

have been developed to do the job more easily and reliably. All that I know operate by the same basic principle illustrated in Figure 11.5. A fabric tube, net, or series of tethered rings is used to contain the spinnaker for storage and hoisting. Once the sail is raised and the halyard secured, a secondary halyard built into the spinnaker handling assembly is used to lift the device to the head of the spinnaker, exposing the sail. Fabric devices corrugate as they are lifted to the head of the spinnaker; those consisting of a series of rings are pushed into a compact stack.

When a spinnaker take-down is desired, a second control line is used to pull the handling assembly down over the sail, funneling and enclosing it. Although usually used with cruising spinnakers, these devices will also handle conventional ones.

12 You and Your Sailmaker

MOST sailors sail for recreation, and most sails are purchased for recreational purposes. However, a prospective sail purchaser is best advised to leave the "let's get away from it all" philosophy behind when he or she walks through a sail loft door. Sailmakers are in business to make a living, and a sail purchase should be approached with the same attitude as any other business transaction. To assume that the sailmaker is casually making a livelihood from what really amounts to his or her hobby is, in most cases, a misapprehension. In reality, sailmaking has become an extremely competitive field in which both unseen benefits and pitfalls can await a naive consumer. To better appreciate the situation, it helps to try to eye the sailing scene from a sailmaker's point of view.

SAILMAKING AS A BUSINESS

One of the most striking features of the sailmaking industry is the large number of small firms—shops employing from one to five people—that have managed to stay in business and even to prosper. There are four principal reasons for the abundance and success of small sail lofts: the low capital cost of starting in the business; the ready availability of keen, young sailors as low-priced, skilled labor; the seasonal aspect of the work; and the fact that most sail purchasers expect and require a great deal of personalized service. Let's look at these factors individually.

To start a sail loft at the most basic level requires only a sewing machine, a few rolls of cloth, some thread and basic hardware, and access to enough uninterrupted floor area for layouts. In some cases, the starting capital has been raised entirely from customers' deposits on a handful of initial sail orders! The low cost of the "entry fee" makes sailmaking accessible and attractive to a comparatively large number of serious sailors who feel they would like to make a living in the recreational marine trades.

Sailmaking is appealing in other ways as well. The work is clean, somewhat less monotonous than most manufacturing jobs, and almost invariably involves lots and lots of sailing. Many talented, enthusiastic young racing sailors find this combination attractive enough so that they are willing to work for remarkably low wages. Of course, a low wage scale, and hence reduced overhead, is an asset to any business, big or small (from an owner's point of view). However, small sail lofts need extremely versatile employees, whereas large sailmaking firms can, and in many cases do, train non-sailors from the general work force to perform specialized, repetitive tasks. The availability of skilled, yet inexpensive, all-around sailmaking help eliminates one of the principal advantages normally associated with manufacturing on a large scale: substantial savings stemming from employee specialization and automation.

Sailmaking in most of the world is seasonal work in the sense that there is a lot more business in the spring and early summer than during the rest of the year. Fall is a particularly tough time for many sailmakers. Unfortunately, it is a business necessity to keep the doors open more or less year round in order to retain a faithful clientele. Here again, smaller lofts with minimal overhead and a versatile staff can realize a competitive advantage.

Many sails are custom items, individually planned during discussions with customers. Even buyers of stock and semistock sails frequently desire and receive personal attention from their sailmakers, often in the form of sailing sessions. In comparison to small sail lofts, large ones generally use more automated production procedures and keep fewer expert sailors on the staff relative to the number of sails manufactured. Of course, this means that on the average, a large sailmaking firm will probably be unable to devote as much consultation time to each individual customer as a small loft can.

NETWORKS AND FRANCHISES

Naturally, there are some advantages to size—the very existence of large sailmaking firms proves as much. A large sailmaker, like any large manufacturer, can cut costs through bulk material purchases, sophisticated production methods, and worker specialization. In sailmaking, the most successful way to realize these benefits, while at the same time retaining most of the advantages of small lofts, is to develop associations consisting of local sailmakers from different geographic areas. These sailmaking networks can consist either of a series of individual lofts wholly, or more commonly, partly owned by a controlling central company; or local lofts bound by contract to a franchiser.

Regardless of how they are set up, most sailmaking networks are basically similar. Advertising costs are ordinarily shared, permitting expensive campaigns that no independent shop could possibly afford. Other shared promotional efforts can include seminars, films, videotapes, newsletters, and major racing programs.

Associations of lofts are able to fund elaborate research and development programs in order to improve sail design and sailmaking techniques. Most of the computer technology associated with contemporary sailmaking has been developed by multiloft networks, either through central research and development groups, or as a result of pooling ideas.

Lofts that are working together can specialize. Thus one can concentrate on certain one-design classes and types of offshore boats, while others take on different assignments.

Finally, associated lofts can work together to even out production loads. Sail ordering patterns are seldom uniform or completely predictable. If one loft finds itself temporarily swamped with work, it is handy to be able to farm some out to associated lofts.

A recent development in the organization of sailmaking networks is the tendency to centralize production in a few large, highly efficient facilities, while relying on local sales and service lofts to liaison with customers. In some cases, these production plants have been situated in countries where labor is substantially less expensive than in Western Europe and North America. Of course, the toughest problem faced by these organizations is the development of communication and transportation systems that will permit sails to be built to particular specifications and delivered without delay.

BUYING SAILS INTELLIGENTLY

The main thrust of this book has been to provide you, the sail user, with a practical understanding of sail function, design, and construction. By spending some time studying with a critical eye the sails you see out on the water, and by talking to experienced local sailors, you should be able to come up with a pretty good idea of what you want and whom to buy from when it comes time to make a purchase.

In purchasing sails directly from a sailmaker (as opposed to obtaining them through a new or used boat purchase), you are actually shopping for more than fabric and hardware. Sailmaker's advice, onboard consultation, guarantees, delivery dates, price and financial terms should all be regarded as part of the package. These items can either be bargaining points, or "mandatory options." In any case, they ultimately affect the value of the purchase; hence should not be overlooked or taken for granted.

The potential value of a sailmaker's advice should not be underestimated. A competent, experienced sailmaker will be able to give you a fair-minded assessment of your future needs that will, in most cases, come pretty close to the optimal balance betewen economy and satisfactory sailing performance for your particular circumstances. In my experience, most individual sailmakers try hard to assess existing inventories objectively, and lean over backwards to avoid appearing too critical of competitors' products.* Sailmaking success depends heavily on repeat business which in turn demands customer satisfaction. The profit potential of the work is too small to attract or hold the attention of quick buck artists.

Onboard consultation with a sailmaker can be extremely valuable. In many cases, sailing sessions are actively solicited by knowledgeable sail buyers as part of the purchase agreement. It is also a touchy subject with many sailmakers, because sailing with customers is extremely time-consuming, and tends to wipe out evenings and weekends. An onboard consultation ordinarily combines a sail inspection with an advanced sailing lesson.

Since many sailmakers are also topnotch sailboat racers,

*The advertising campaigns of the major sailmaking organizations are frequently less discreet.

they are often sought after to crew on customers' boats. Because most sailmakers wish to preserve amateur status (I.Y.R.U. Appendix 1), they take pains to avoid any suggestion that they are being paid to engage in racing. Therefore, when a sailmaker agrees to come aboard for a race, it's best to regard this simply as a gesture of friendship and a chance for some after-hours fun.

Sailmakers' guarantees can range from vague assurances of satisfaction to point by point agreements to rectify specific deficiencies if they occur within particular periods of time. Here the best advice is simply to evaluate the guarantee being offered in light of what you know is most likely to be wrong (or to go wrong) with a sail. Questioning sailors who have dealt with various sailmakers can help you form an opinion regarding the reliability of their guarantees.

Delivery dates on sail orders tend to cause considerable aggravation to customers and sailmakers alike. Customers often hold onto their deposit money until the eleventh hour before placing their orders, while sailmakers are sometimes prone to "promise the world" in order to ensure getting an order. Here, mutual understanding can go a long way toward avoiding hassles. It's also a good idea for a potential customer to ask other sailors about the delivery track record of the sailmaker(s) he is considering.

Sail prices, like the prices of anything else, mean little unless evaluated in terms of the other characteristics that determine the value of the prospective purchase. However, having read this far, you should be in a reasonably good position to assess the cost-to-value relationships of different sailmakers' offerings. Seasonal discounts, whole inventory discounts, group or fleet discounts, and any number of other price inducements have been and will continue to be used by sailmakers to woo customers.

Standard payment terms in the sailmaking industry are a

50 percent deposit when the order is placed, with the balance due upon delivery. The relatively large deposit is the sailmaker's assurance that the customer will not back out of the deal leaving him with a completed sail that can be difficult or impossible to resell. Nevertheless, sailmakers are sometimes willing to accept smaller deposits, particularly if business is slow and the particular sail in question is a popular item. Likewise, some sailmakers may be willing to extend credit to certain of their regular customers—private individuals as well as yacht dealers, brokers, and boat builders.

THE EMOTIONAL SIDE OF SAIL BUYING

Regrettably, not all sail purchases are the result of rational decision. Racing sailors are particularly prone to buying sails on impulse, or out of desperation, although cruising sailors are by no means immune to similar motivations. Racers who are dissatisfied with their performances will, in many cases, buy a brand of sails other than that favored by the class leaders in hopes of achieving a speed breakthrough. More surprising still, although the hoped-for breakthrough often fails to materialize, these sailors not infrequently return to the same sailmaker to try again for that breakthrough. From an objective viewpoint, it makes sense to buy sails like those used by the most successful competitors in one's class, but it is human nature to seek a tangible advantage, no matter how elusive.

The sale of racing sails is, to a large extent, promoted by racing success. As a conscious decision, it makes some sense to select a sailmaker with a proven record—the odds of getting a satisfactory sail are somewhat improved. Of course, racing victories sell sails on a subconscious level as well. To keep things in perspective, it is vital to remember that boat preparation, crew work, strategy, and tactics are each as important, if not more important, than sails in determining race outcomes. An ace crew can make even mediocre sails look pretty good (although top sailors won't put up with iffy sails for long). Again, however, human nature being what it is, sailmakers recognize the extreme desirability of putting their sails on the best-sailed boats in important events and assisting these favored competitors with additional sailing expertise in so far as possible.

Strong opinions and cherished beliefs not infrequently hinder both cruising sailors and racing sailors from making rational decisions about their sails. To avoid becoming handicapped in this way, just ask yourself whether what you've heard or what you're thinking really makes sense. Don't be blinded by authority. Old Joe Salt may have cruised to Tahiti and back in 1956, but does his background necessarily mean he's right when he tells you that "pressed-in rings are no damn good and roller furling is designed to drown sailors"?

CUSTOMER COOPERATION IN SAILMAKING

The role of the customer should not end with paying the bills. A sailor who takes an active role in the planning of his or her sails is much more likely to be satisfied with the results than one who leaves everything to the sailmaker. The customer can be of particular assistance in checking that the rig dimensions and details in the hands of the sailmaker are absolutely correct for his particular boat. Most sailmakers prefer to measure boats themselves if the boat is accessible to them, but few will object to receiving a second set of measurements obtained independently as a double check.

After a new sail is in use, most sailmakers greatly appreciate knowledgeable feedback regarding the shape and other characteristics of the sail. Sail photographs as described in Chapter 3 are particularly useful. By going to the trouble to follow through the sail purchase in these ways, the customer can do himself as well as the sailmaker a favor. Customers who provide good feedback and cultivate a solid working relationship with their sailmakers are uncommon enough that many sailmakers will go out of their way to accommodate them.

Glossary

AFT Toward the stern of a vessel.

AIRFOIL An object, usually curved in cross section, that is designed to produce lift when situated in a stream of moving air.

ANGLE OF ATTACK The angle made by the chord of a sail and the apparent wind. Note that angle of attack is not synonymous with ENTRY ANGLE.

APPARENT WIND The wind produced by the combination of the true wind blowing over the water and the "induced wind" created by the forward motion of the boat. The apparent wind is the wind you feel while aboard a sailboat under way, as well as being the wind to which the sails react.

ASPECT RATIO The ratio of height to girth in a sail or other airfoil. A high-aspect sail has a long luff and a short foot. For a low-aspect one, the two are somewhat closer in length, although aspect ratios less than two to one are extremely rare for modern sailing rigs.

ATHWARTSHIPS Toward the sides of a hull or deck.

BACKSTAY A wire running from the mast to the stern that helps prevent the mast from falling forward.

BACKWIND The deflection of wind (downwash) caused by a sail or sailboat as it affects another sail or boat behind. A headsail is said to backwind a mainsail when its downwash deflects the luff of the main to windward. One sailboat backwinds another when the downwash from its sails impinges on the latter.

BACKWIND ZONE See SAFE LEEWARD POSITION.

BALANCED WEAVE A cloth whose warp and fill yarns are equal or almost equal in size.

BANANA STAYSAIL A full, lightweight staysail tacked to the weather rail and used in conjunction with a spinnaker on broad reaches and runs.

BATTEN A stiff, narrow strip or rod used to support the leech of a sail.

BATTEN POCKET An elongated space containing a batten made by sewing the edges of strip of sailcloth to the surface of a sail.

BEAM REACH A course with the apparent wind on the beam or at right angles to the boat's progress.

BERNOULLI'S PRINCIPLE The pressure within a mass of moving fluid is inversely related to flow velocity. This fundamental law of fluid dynamics was first described by Daniel Bernoulli in 1738.

BIAS At an orientation of approximately 45° to the threadlines of a woven fabric.

BLACK BANDS High-visibility marks on the spars of racing boats denoting allowable limits for the extension of sails.

BLADE Common term for a high-aspect jib that just fills a boat's foretriangle.

BLOCK A sheave or pulley contained in a housing and used to turn or deflect a line or rope while minimizing the friction that might otherwise prevent the line from running freely.

BLOOPER A very full, lightweight genoa made from nylon spinnaker cloth that is flown alongside the spinnaker and to leeward of the headstay on broad reaches and runs.

BOOM A horizontal spar free to pivot athwartships that is used to hold the clew of a sail outboard.

BOUNDARY LAYER The region close to the surface of an object immersed in a moving fluid where frictional forces retard flow to some extent.

BROAD REACH A course with the apparent wind aft of the beam, but not dead astern.

BROADSEAM An overlapping seam whose width varies to create the effect of slightly tapering two adjacent panels in the sail. Broadseams are used to increase or, occasionally, to reduce the three-dimensional curvature of sails.

CALENDARING A sailcloth finishing procedure that involves crushing the woven material between heated steel rollers.

CAMBER The curvature or concavity of a sail as it might be viewed in horizontal cross section. Also known as draft or flow.

CAMBER DISTRIBUTION The overall, three-dimensional shape of a sail. Camber distribution is usually described by measuring the camber ratio at three or more heights in a sail.

CAMBER RATIO The depth of a sail at some particular height divided by the chord at that height.

CAT KETCH A no-headsail rig consisting of a mainsail set on the forward mast and a comparatively large mizzen on the aft mast.

CAT RIG A single-masted rig that employs no sails other than a mainsail.

CENTER OF EFFORT The "balancing point" where all the forces acting on a sail or sailing rig have the net effect of a single combined force.

CENTER OF GRAVITY The point within (or near) an object around which all parts of the object exactly balance each other.

CHAFE Damage caused by repeatedly rubbing against something.

CHEEK BLOCK A block with a flush base intended for permanent mounting on a deck or spar.

CHORD The straight-line horizontal path from the luff of sail to the leech. A chord line bridges the camber of the sail.

CLEVIS PIN A metal fastening designed to slip into a hole and withstand sheer loads.

CLEW The corner of a sail where the leech intersects with the foot.

CLOSE HAULED Sailing a course with the sails sheeted fairly far inboard to provide optimal upwind progress.

CLOSE REACH A course that puts the angle of apparent wind forward of the beam, but as not far forward as when sailing close hauled.

CLOSED LEECHED See TIGHT LEECHED.

COMPOUND RIGS Rigs such as sloops, cutters, and ketches, characterized by having two or more sails set in a row with one or more slots between them.

CRIMP The zigzag paths taken by the yarns comprising a woven material as they alternately pass over and under one another.

CRINGLE An "eye" or reinforced hole in a sail used as an attachment point for lines, clevis pins, or shackles.

CROSS CUT See HORIZONTAL CUT.

CROSS FLOW The passage of wind at an upward slant past a sail or diagonally under the foot of a sail.

CRUISING SPINNAKER An asymmetrical spinnaker designed to be set without a spinnaker pole.

CUNNINGHAM HOLE A cringle inserted a short distance above the tack of a sail through which a control line is passed. While sailing, tension can be applied to the entire length of the luff above the Cunningham hole without making the overall luff length of the sail any longer than it was to start with. This invention is credited to race car driver and sailor Briggs Cunningham.

CURL Undesirable curvature or folding over of the luff of a spinnaker or the leech of any sail.

CUTTER RIG A single-masted sailing rig that routinely uses two headsails, a jib set on the outer headstay, and a staysail on the inner headstay.

CUTTING The step in sailmaking where lengths of sailcloth

are measured off and cut from a roll to become the panels of a sail.

CUTTING TABLE A standing-height worktable, usually equipped with a measuring grid and curved stenciling lines, which is used in some sail lofts to roll out and cut sail panels one at a time.

DACRON® DuPont trade name for polyester in the form of strands or yarns.

DARN Repair technique employing a looping stitch to pull together and secure the opposite sides of a tear.

DAZY STAYSAIL A very light, high-clewed staysail of about 90 percent LP, which can either be tacked behind the forestay for use under a spinnaker, or at the front of the foretriangle as a drifter for extremely light-air racing.

DECK-SWEEPER A headsail whose foot contacts or nearly contacts the deck for most of its length to prevent the flow of air under the foot with an attendant increase in induced drag.

DEPTH The perpendicular distance from a chord to the deepest point on the cambered surface of the sail at that height.

DEPTH TO CHORD RATIO See CAMBER RATIO.

DIVIDED RIG Any sailing rig with two or more masts.

DOUBLE-HEADED RIG The use of two headsails at the same time, either aboard a true cutter or on a sloop, yawl, or ketch that sets a staysail in conjunction with a genoa or a jib.

DOWNWASH Deflection of flow downstream of a airfoil, sail, or other lift-generating shape. Downwash is so named because the air passing the trailing edge of an airplane wing is deflected toward the earth below.

DRAFT See CAMBER.

DRAFT AFT Sail with maximum depth located comparatively far back (generally aft of about 44 percent).

DRAFT FORWARD Sail with maximum depth located comparatively close to the luff.

DRIFTER A headsail for very light winds.

D-RING A metal fitting shaped like the letter *D*, which is attached with lengths of nylon webbing to the clews, heads, or tacks of some sails to permit sheets, halyards, or shackles to be secured.

DUAL STAYSAIL A sail intended both for use under a spinnaker on broad reaches and in conjunction with a genoa for close reaching.

E MEASUREMENT Either the length of a mainsail foot or, in the case of a racing boat, the distance from the aft face of the mast to the clew-limiting black band near the outboard end of the boom.

EASE To slack off a sheet, halyard, or other control line.

ENDPLATE A flat, perpendicular flow barrier affixed to one end of a wing, sail, or fin that reduces tip vortex formation and induced drag. (See DECK-SWEEPER.)

ENTRY ANGLE The angle made by the center line of a boat and the luff of a close-hauled headsail as viewed from above. Entry angle is the principal determinant of pointing ability, but not, in most cases, of upwind sailing efficiency.

FAIRING Any technique for smoothing out irregularities in a line or surface.

FANNING Sailmakers' technique for making one edge of a three-dimensionally curved sail lie flat on the floor. An S-shaped fold or undulation is "thrown" into the sail parallel to the edge (luff, leech, or foot) that is being prepared for trimming.

FILL The yarns that run from side to side in a roll of cloth.

FINISHING Procedures used to improve the qualities of greige goods and turn them into sailcloth.

FINS The keel and rudder of a modern sailboat.

FLAT SAIL A sail with little camber.

FLATTENING REEF A shallow slab reef utilizing a single reefing cringle a short distance up the leech from the clew. Using the flattening reef has the same effect as pulling the clew beyond the black band (or boom end) using the outhaul.

FLOW See CAMBER. Also the bulk movement of fluid.

FLOW SEPARATION See STALL.

FLUID A substance, gas, or liquid, that has no fixed shape.

FLUTTER TEST Method of testing sailcloth that mimics the effects of luffing or ragging a sail while on the water. After several cloth specimens have been fluttered in an air stream under standardized conditions, stress-strain tests are conducted to determine how far its mechanical properties have deteriorated.

FLYING SHAPE The actual cambered shape assumed by a sail while in use.

FOLD In addition to the everyday meaning of this word, it is used to describe a pronounced curl in the luff of an undertrimmed spinnaker.

FOOT The edge of a sail extending from the tack to the clew.

FOOT LINE A light line inside the foot tabling (hem).

FOOT ROACH See FOOT ROUND.

FORETRIANGLE The space bounded by the forestay, foredeck, and front face of the mast.

FRACTIONAL RIG A sloop rig with a foretriangle height (I measurement) that is only a fraction the total height of the mast.

FREE-LUFF SAIL Any sail whose luff is not mechanically attached to a spar or stay.

FREE-STREAM FLOW Movement of fluid when unimpeded by the presence of any object in the stream.

FULL SAIL A sail with a lot of camber. Opposite of a FLAT SAIL.

GENOA A headsail large enough to overlap the mainsail.

GIRTH The horizontal measurement from luff to leech along the surface of a sail.

GOOSENECK An articulating fitting that attaches the boom to the mast.

GREIGE GOODS Cloth as it comes off the loom.

GROMMET A fitting used to make a small eye or cringle in a sail, tarpaulin, or cover.

HALYARD A line used to hoist a sail.

HAND The texture and handling qualities of a sailcloth.

HANDWORKED RING A cringle or eye that is made by stitching around the perimeter of a metal ring. A thin metal liner is then bent over the inside of the ring to protect the stitching.

HEAD The intersection of the luff and leech at the top of a sail.

HEADBOARD A metal or plastic plate used to stiffen the head of a sail.

HEADSAIL A sail with a fairly straight luff that is set forward of the forward mast.

HEADSTAY A wire rope or extruded aluminum foil extending from the bow to the front face of the mast at near the masthead.

HEADSTAY FOIL A grooved extrusion that envelopes or replaces the headstay and accepts headsail luff tapes.

HEADSTAY SAG The lateral and rearward deflection of a headstay caused by the aerodynamic lifting forces generated by the headsail set on that stay.

HEAT SETTING Sailcloth finishing technique employing high temperatures to shrink and tighten the weave.

HEEL Tendency of a sailboat to tip laterally under the influence of aerodynamic and hydrodynamic forces.

HEELING FORCES The lateral components of the forces generated by sails, rig components, or underwater parts of sailboats.

HIGH SLEY A term for a fabric whose warp yarns are larger and less crimped than its fill yarns.

HORIZONTAL CUT Layout pattern for a sail in which the panels run perpendicularly to the leech.

HOT KNIFE Sailmakers' tool that cuts synthetic sailcloth by melting the material with an electrically heated blade.

I MEASUREMENT Vertical distance from the point where the

forestay intersects with the mast down to the sheer line of the boat.

INDUCED DRAG Drag created as a direct consequence of the generation of lift.

INNER FORESTAY A second shorter forestay aft of the primary one that is used to support the luff of the staysail on a cutter-rigged boat.

IOR International Offshore Rule; currently the most popular rating rule for handicap racing in offshore yachts.

J MEASUREMENT Horizontal distance from the point where the forestay intersects with the deck aft to the front face of the mast.

JIB A headsail that fits inside the foretriangle without overlapping the mast.

KEEL A large fin on the bottom of a sailboat that serves the dual function of providing lift to counterbalance lifting forces from the sails and housing ballast.

KEVLAR® A plastic belonging to the aramid group developed by DuPont for use in automobile tires and possessing very favorable strength-to-weight characteristics.

LAPPER A headsail that overlaps the mainsail just slightly.

LATERAL FORCE See HEELING FORCES.

LAYOUT Step in sailmaking procedures in which the panels of a sail are arranged full scale on the sail-loft floor.

LEAD ANGLE The angle between the sheet extending downward from the clew of a sail, and a horizontal plane.

LEADING EDGE The upstream edge of a three-dimensional airfoil.

LEADING EDGE SEPARATION BUBBLE An area just behind the luff on the leeward side of a sail where the wind breaks away from the sail's surface before dropping back to the sail's contours farther aft.

LEECH The unsupported edge of a sail extending from the head to the clew. The leech constitutes the trailing edge of an airfoil.

LEECH FALL-OFF Fault in which the leech of the sail drops away to leeward giving the camber of the sail an S-shaped profile.

LEECH FLUTTER Tendency for a strip of sailcloth close to the leech to oscillate rapidly from side to side, causing accelerated wear and an annoying noise.

LEECH TENSION Stress induced in the part of a sail bordering the leech by a combination of aerodynamic loading and downward trimming forces.

LEECHLINE A light line inside the leech tabling (hem).

LEEWARD The opposite (or approximately opposite) of the direction from which the wind is blowing.

LEEWAY Tendency of most boats to sideslip slightly when sailing close-hauled or on a close reach.

LET-OUT A small reduction in panel taper made by unstitching part of a broadseam and reassembling the seam with less seam overlap.

LIFT A force, acting at right angles to the axis of flow, that is created when flow is diverted by an asymmetrically shaped object.

LIFT/DRAG RATIO The relationship between magnitude of lifting forces versus drag forces generated by a sailing rig or other airfoil in a particular set of flow conditions.

LIFTING FORCE See LIFT.

LINE A cord, rope, or wire serving a specific function aboard a sailboat.

LOAD An everyday language synonym for STRESS.

LOFT See SAIL LOFT.

LP MEASUREMENT The perpendicular distance (shortest measurement) from the clew to the luff of a headsail. Also sometimes referred to as LPG (Longest Perpendicular Girth).

LUFF As a noun, the edge of the sail extending from head to tack. As a verb, the fluttering or deflection to windward of a sail that is trimmed to an excessively small angle of attack.

LUFF CURVE The convex, concave, or S-shaped profile of the luff of a sail.

LUFF SOCK A tubular fabric device used to encase a furled headsail when it is not in use to protect it from sun and weather.

LUFF TENSION Stress applied to the sailcloth comprising the luff area of a sail, either by raising the halyard, or by pulling down on the tack or a Cunningham hole.

MAINSAIL The sail whose luff is attached to the mast or, in the case of a divided rig, to the main mast.

MAST In sailing terminology, a spar used to support sails.

MASTHEAD RIG A sailing rig characterized by a headstay that extends to the very top of the mast.

MAXIMUM DEPTH LOCATION The point along the length of a chord where perpendicular distance to the surface of the sail is greatest.

MELAMINE A plastic resin used to impregnate and stabilize some woven sailcloths.

MESSINGER LINE A light cord placed inside a hem or tabling that is subsequently used to pull a larger line or rope into place.

MITER Seam joining two distinct parts of a sail. For example, the miter seam in a tri-radial spinnaker joins the port and starboard radial clew sections.

MIZZEN A sail whose luff is attached to the shorter, secondary mast (mizzen mast) that is stepped aft of the main mast aboard a ketch or yawl.

MOLDED SHAPE The shape a sail assumes when suspended horizontally indoors (in the absence of wind loading).

MULE A heavy-weather overlapping headsail with a luff that is considerably shorter than the forestay.

MYLAR® DuPont trade name for polyester in sheet or film form.

NEGATIVE BROADSEAM A tapered seam that overlaps more in the middle than toward the luff and the leech. Used to reduce camber.

NYLON A familiar synthetic used in the sailmaking trade for spinnaker and manufacture.

OPEN LEECHED Sail that is flat, draft forward, and highly twisted.

OUTBOARD Strictly speaking, outside the perimeter of the deck. Sometimes used casually to mean remote from the centerline of a boat.

OUTBOARD REEFING LINE Slab reefing line used to draw the reefing clew down to the boom.

OUTHAUL Control used to apply tension to the foot of a mainsail or mizzen.

OVERLAP Portion of a genoa that extends aft of the mast.

P MEASUREMENT Either the actual length of the mainsail luff, or the distance between the black bands on the mast of a racing boat that delimit maximum allowable mainsail luff length.

PANELS The individual strips of sailcloth that are sewn together to make a sail.

PEEL TEST Measurement of the force required to strip apart the components of a laminated sailcloth.

PISTON HANK A hook-shaped fitting with a sliding gate that is used to attach the luff of a headsail to the forestay.

PLOTTER See X-Y PLOTTER.

POLYESTER Synthetic most commonly used in the manufacture of sails because of its strength, low-stretch properties, and modest cost.

POROSITY TEST Measurement of the rate that air leaks through a sailcloth.

PRESSED-IN RING Cringles that are set into place using a hydraulic press.

PRESSURE DRAG Drag force resulting from a pressure difference between the upstream (high pressure) side of a flow obstruction and its downstream (low pressure) side.

PRESSURE GRADIENT A progressive increase or decrease in pressure over a distance.

RADIAL CONSTRUCTION Layout pattern in which a series of more-or-less triangular panels radiate from a head, tack, or clew.

RAG Easing sheet or turning the boat into the wind so its sail(s) luff and flutter like a flag in the wind.

REACH Any sailing course other than close hauled or running before the wind.

REEF Method used to reduce the area of a sail to keep the boat from being overpowered in strong winds.

REEFING CLEW A clew cringle and associated reinforcing patch some distance up the leech, which becomes the clew when the sail is reefed.

REEFING TACK A tack cringle some distance up the luff, which is secured to the or other tack fitting when reefing.

REEFING TIES Short ribbons or lines used to secure a reef.

RESIN COATING Plastic coating or "filler" applied to a woven sailcloth to lock the weave into place and improve its stretch resistance.

RESIN IMPREGNATION Saturation of a weave with a solution of plastic resin, which is then induced to harden, stabilizing the resulting sailcloth.

RIP STOP Weave pattern in which larger yarns are introduced at intervals to serve as barriers to the propagation of tears.

ROACH Extra sail area outside a straight line from head to clew.

ROLLER FURLING Stowing a sail by wrapping it up around a rotating luff wire or luff extrusion.

ROLLER REEFING Technique for altering mainsail area by spooling the foot of the mainsail onto a boom that can be mechanically rotated.

RUN Sailing with the apparent wind directly or almost directly astern.

SAFE LEEWARD POSITION Slightly ahead and to leeward of another sailboat.

SAIL LOFT Shop where sails are made. Traditionally these

were usually on the top floors of commercial buildings, hence the name.

SAILCLOTH A fabric specifically intended for sailmaking.

SAUSAGE BAG Elongated sack with a zipper down the side used to stow headsails on modern offshore racing boats so that they will be ready for fast headsail changes.

SEAMING Process of sewing or glueing together the panels of a sail.

SECOND LAYOUT Step in sailmaking in which the assembled panels are laid out again on the loft floor to trim the luff, leech, and foot.

SELVAGE GUIDE LINES Machine-made marks parallel to the trimmed edges on rolls of commercial sailcloths that provide a standard seam overlap and a basis for broadseaming.

SHACKLE A U-shaped metal fitting with a removable pin spanning its ends, which is used as a fastening link.

SHEER FORCE Internal stress tangential to the surface of a body or structure. A sheer force tends to make parts slide past one another.

SHEER LINE Curvature of the edge of the deck as viewed from the side.

SHEET A control line extending aft and down from the clew of a sail. Also the act of hauling in such a line.

SHEET LEAD Block or fairlead attached to the hull or deck that governs the sheeting angle and lead angle of a headsail or spinnaker.

SHEET TENSION The magnitude of the pull on a sheet.

SHEETING ANGLE Horizontal angle between a boat's midline and a line connecting the sheet-lead position with the tack of a particular sail.

SHORT SHEET Temporary sheet used to keep a headsail drawing while the two long primary sheets are attached to the clew of a replacement headsail in preparation for a sail change on an offshore racing boat.

SHROUDS Rigging wires used to support a mast from side to side.

SKIN FRICTION See VISCOUS DRAG.

SLAB REEFING Modern technique for reducing sail area by transferring sailing loads to a secondary tack/clew pair located some distance above the sail's foot.

SLIDE Metal or plastic fitting that fits over a track or into a slot on the side of a spar and to which the luff of a sail is, in turn, attached.

SLOOP Popular single-masted sailing rig that characteristically utilizes just one sail set forward of the mast at any given time.

SLOT The space separating two sails; most commonly a mainsail and a headsail.

SLOTTED RIG See COMPOUND RIG.

SLUG Special subclass of sail slides that fit into a rounded groove with a keyhole-shaped cross section.

SPAR A mast or boom.

SPINNAKER Large, lightweight sail with three free edges used on reaches and runs.

SPINNAKER CADDIE Device for compacting and securing a spinnaker to make it easier to set and douse.

SPINNAKER POLE Strut used to hold the tack of a spinnaker away from the mast.

SPREADERS Struts used to hold stays away from a mast so that they meet the mast at a more favorable angle.

SPUR GROMMET Small cringle comprised of a toothed ring and an interlocking collar that are assembled in a die with a blow from a mallet.

STALL Stoppage or reversal in the flow of fluid along one face of an airfoil, resulting in loss of lift and a dramatic increase in drag.

STARCUT SPINNAKER Spinnaker design in which a radial head and two radial clews all meet in the body of the sail.

STAYS Rigging wires supporting a mast fore and aft.

STAYSAIL A headsail set a short distance aft of another headsail or a spinnaker.

STEM The extreme bow of a boat.

STORM JIB A small, heavily constructed headsail used for very strong winds.

STRAIN Bending, stretching or other deformation of an object as a result of a stress force or forces.

STRESS Force or forces acting on an object.

STRESS/STRAIN TEST A measurement or series of measurements of the deformation that a sample undergoes when stressed.

STRETCH Strain caused by tensile force(s).

SUN STRIP Strip of opaque fabric attached to the leech and foot of a furling sail to prevent ultraviolet light from damaging the body of the sail when it is not in use.

TABLING A hem at the edge of a sail made by folding the fabric over one or more times and sewing the folds into place.

TACK The corner of a sail where the luff meets the foot. Also used to refer to the side of the boat from which the wind is blowing, e.g., "port tack," as well as the maneuver employed to change from one tack to the other by turning the boat through the eye of the wind.

TAKE-UP A small increase in panel taper created by unstitching one end of a seam and reassembling it with more seam overlap.

TALLBOY A high-aspect staysail primarily intended to set inside a genoa for close reaching, but acceptable for use under a spinnaker.

TAPE Narrow strip of sailcloth used to hem the edges of some sails.

TELLTALE Ribbons or short lengths of woolen yarn fastened to the surface of a sail at one end and used as visual indicators of air flow direction and stability.

TENSION A pulling force.

TERELENE® British trade name for polyester in yarn or fiber form.

THREADLINE The orientation of yarns in a woven fabric.

TIGHT LEECHED Sail that is full and draft aft with minimal twist.

TIP VORTEX Spiraling turbulence pattern generated by cross flow over the end or sloped trailing edge of an airfoil.

TRAILING EDGE The downstream edge of a sail or other airfoil.

TRAVELLER A sliding device used to control the athwartships position of a sheet lead.

TRIM Adjustments of shape and orientation aimed at improving sailing performance.

TRI-RADIAL SPINNAKER A spinnaker design pattern featuring a radial head and two radial clews separated by several horizontal panels.

TRUE WIND Wind speed and direction as perceived by an observer who is motionless with respect to the earth.

TRYSAIL A small, heavily constructed mainsail designed to be substituted for the normal main in storm conditions.

TURBULENCE Erratic, disturbed flow.

TWIST Tendency for the upper portions of a sail to operate at angles of attack rather than parts of the sail farther below.

UNA RIG Sophisticated cat rig utilizing a pivoting airfoil mast and, in most cases, full-length battens.

UNBALANCED WEAVE Fabric in which the yarns comprising one threadline are larger and less crimped than those of the other.

UNSTAYED RIG Rig based on a spar that stands without the aid of shrouds or stays.

UPWASH The deflection of approaching fluid toward the low-pressure side of an airfoil situated slightly downstream.

URETHANE Plastic commonly used in applying resin coatings to sailcloth.

VANG Mechanical device used to apply a downward pull on a mainsail boom as means of adjusting leech tension and twist.

VERTICAL CUT Sail layout pattern in which the panels parallel the leech.

VISCOUS DRAG Drag associated with frictional sheer forces between a surface and the fluid moving past it.

WAKE A turbulent zone downstream of a flow obstruction.

WARP Threadline parallel to the length of a roll of sailcloth.

WASH TEST Measurements of the change in mechanical characteristics of a sailcloth sample caused by wetting and abrasion.

WINDWARD The direction from which the wind blows.

WING SAIL A thick, rigid airfoil used to propel a sailing vessel, buggy, or ice boat.

X-Y PLOTTER A machine capable of moving a stylus or cutting tool both transversely and laterally under precise control.

YARN One of the longitudinal or transverse elements in a weave.

YIELD Permanent stretch of a sailcloth caused by overload.

YIELD POINT The amount of stress on a standard sailcloth sample that begins to induce permanent deformation as indicated by a pronounced increase in the slope of the stress/strain graph.

Further Readings

COMPREHENSIVE REFERENCES

HOWARD-WILLIAMS, JEREMY. *Sails*. London: Adlard Coles, Ltd., 1967. Age not withstanding, this is a valuable sourcebook. Portions have been updated, although the sections on theory, sailcloth, and sail design are hardly "state-of-the-art." Still, there are more constants than variables in the sailing world and Howard-Williams does a good job of explaining them.

ROSS, WALLACE. *Sail Power*. New York: Alfred A. Knopf, Inc., 1973. Still the most exhaustive available source of information on sails, sailhandling gear, and trimming techniques. Although ten years old, most of the book remains current. An important reference for the serious sailor.

SAILMAKING AND SAIL REPAIR

BLANFORD, PERCY. *Modern Sailmaking*. Blue Ridge Summit, Pa.: Tab Books, 1979. In light of the huge number of books addressed to the aspiring boatbuilder, it is surprising that more sailmaking texts are not available. This is among the better in a meager crop. Some fundamental points are oversimplified, but the techniques sections that constitute the guts of the book are useful and detailed.

HOWARD-WILLIAMS, JEREMY. *The Care and Repair of Sails.* Boston: Sail Books Inc., 1976. Covers just about everything an amateur should know to maintain and modify sails. At least as good a guidebook for home sailmaking as any of the "do-it-yourself" manuals I've seen. Also includes excellent sections on diagnosing and rectifying faults.

SCHMIT, BILL. *Sailmaking.* New York: Drake Publishers Inc., 1976. A satisfactory primer for the beginner who wants to try building a small, simple sail or recutting a used one. Good explanations of basic techniques and many illustrations. Considers broadseaming too difficult for amateurs.

SAILING THEORY AND SAIL FUNCTION

MARCHAJ, C.A. *Aero-hydrodynamics of Sailing.* New York: Dodd, Mead, & Co., 1979. The most detailed, comprehensive book on sailing theory ever written. Written on a level that a technically minded reader lacking formal training in engineering or advanced mathematics can understand, although certain sections can be expected to take time and patience. Some sailing experts disagree with a number of Marchaj's views, but few would dispute that he is the world's foremost authority on sailing theory as well as its leading teacher of this subject.